Chinese Snuff Bottles
The Edward Choate O'Dell Collection

The Asia House Gallery, New York City, November 1982

Chinese Snuff Bottles
The Edward Choate O'Dell Collection

By John Gilmore Ford

With An Essay By Emily Byrne Curtis

Published by The International Chinese Snuff Bottle Society
2601 North Charles Street, Baltimore, Maryland 21218 (USA)
Copyright ©1982 by The International Chinese Snuff Bottle Society
Designed and Printed by Geo. W. King Company, Baltimore, Maryland
Photography by Blakeslee/Lane, Baltimore, Maryland
Library of Congress Catalogue Card Number 82-83402
ISBN 0-9609668-0-3

To
Edward Choate O'Dell
Gentleman, mentor, benefactor, and friend

Contents

Foreword 9

Preface 11

**Edward Choate O'Dell
A Memoir** 13

**Snuff and Chinese Snuff
Bottles: An Historical
View** 19

Catalogue of the Exhibition 27

Bibliography 76

Glossary 78

Foreword

Once again, The Asia Society is happy to serve as the host institution for an Annual Meeting of The International Chinese Snuff Bottle Society. As John Ford mentions in his preface, this occasion is particularly appropriate, because the last time the organization met in New York eleven years ago, it was for its first annual convention and the meetings were held at the original Asia Society's headquarters on 64th Street. Since then, both Societies have grown in scope, membership and influence. The Asia Society has recently come into ownership of a permanent collection of Asian Art, bequeathed to it by John D. Rockefeller 3rd. A new building has just been constructed on Park Avenue to house the collection and better present its many significant activities. This building has now been opened for a year, and it is a pleasure to welcome members of the Society to our new facility on their return visit to New York.

The selection of the Edward Choate O'Dell collection for display is also an event of considerable significance as it is one of the finest groupings of its kind. The collection also contains a large enough number of examples so that, with this careful selection, we can show a wide variety of the styles, shapes, techniques, and materials in which these small, precious objects appear. From study of the material we present, it is not hard to understand why these exquisite containers have been so fascinating and avidly sought after.

Mr. O'Dell was one of the most passionate of an already passionate breed of collectors. The enthusiasm he had for his snuff bottles and his pleasure in anticipating this exhibition and publication are sadly tempered by his death last spring. A more fitting memorial could not be imagined.

The exhibition was the inspiration and work of John Ford who has seen through the many details of publication, selection, shipping and installation. The design of the exhibition was conceived by Cleo Nichols and his staff. On behalf of both The Asia Society and The International Chinese Snuff Bottle Society, we extend our thanks to them.

Allen Wardwell
Director, Asia Society Gallery

Preface

Edward Choate O'Dell was the founder and president of The International Chinese Snuff Bottle Society, which under its original name of The Chinese Snuff Bottle Society of America held its first convention at the Asia Society in New York in 1969. When it was decided to hold the 1982 meeting in New York City with a special program at The Asia Society, the Snuff Bottle Society's board of directors approved a plan to have a major exhibition of the most important bottles from the O'Dell collection as a tribute to him. Mr. O'Dell, who looked forward to the occasion with great enthusiasm, died unexpectedly on March 24, 1982, at the age of 81. The exhibition and this catalogue of it thus serve as a memorial to him.

As Mr. O'Dell owned one of the finest collections amassed in the past fifty years, the only difficulty in the selection process was in deciding what not to show. The choice of bottles for the exhibition was based primarily on quality, in some cases on uniqueness, and on a desire to demonstrate the wide range of materials used by many artists over more than three hundred years to create these miniature masterpieces of Chinese art.

Jade is the first category shown, as it is considered by Chinese scholars and craftsmen to be the single most precious stone. Following the nineteen jade examples is a selection of forty hardstones, including pure rock crystal and the various related stones in the quartz family, as well as more ornate stones such as lapis lazuli, malachite, tourmaline, and sapphire. Next is a group of twenty-two bottles made from organic materials of which the most representative are coral, ivory, amber, hornbill, mammoth tooth, and lacquer. Then come the nine metal bottles, including one of the earliest dated series of bottles known to exist, and eight enamel-decorated metal bottles. The glass category begins with nine richly enamel-decorated examples, followed by ten monochromatic glass bottles, and finally twenty-nine overlaid, embellished, and etched glass bottles. The ceramics are represented by thirty-three specimens of porcelain and Yixing ware. The final category illustrates the last creative outpouring of Chinese art in the form of the inside-painted bottle; twenty-one examples are included here.

The back of the catalogue includes a glossary listing all Chinese words written in Pinyin (a romanization of Chinese words). The older Wade-Giles usage is included along with the English equivalents and the Chinese characters. A bibliography follows which clearly outlines the references used for dating and for the historical and symbolic significance of each bottle. However, as with all research, I have not always agreed with the positions taken by authors of the books listed but have attempted to give reasons for my divergence of opinion.

I first want to thank the board of our society and The Asia Society for their help in all aspects of the preparation of the exhibition and the catalogue. It would not have been possible to perform these tasks without the prior work and assistance of many scholars and friends. First among these is the late Lilla S. Perry. Her book *Chinese Snuff Bottles: The Adventures and Studies of a Collector* was the motivating force for an entire new generation of snuff bottle collectors, including me. I was fortunate to see her when she visited Mr. O'Dell in Baltimore, and to go with him on frequent visits to her home in Los Angeles.

Everyone in the field of snuff bottle scholarship is indebted to Hugh M. Moss. He pioneered research at a time when no one else was truly interested, and inspired the majority of scholarship that has been undertaken in subsequent years. The depth and quality of his work are outstanding. It was he, too, who first voiced the idea of having an exhibition to honor Edward O'Dell.

No one in the snuff bottle world will ever forget the enthusiasm and tenacity of Bob C. Stevens as collector, scholar, and friend. He was the inspiration for many collectors, and his great work, *The Collector's Book of Snuff Bottles,* will remain unexcelled, I am sure, in its range and for the love of snuff bottles projected in every word.

I am indebted to Emily Byrne Curtis for agreeing to write an essay on the origin and history of snuff and snuff bottles. The new documentation which the essay includes will surely benefit future scholars.

Special thanks are due Chaoling and Fong Chow. Mr. Chow is well known as the Far Eastern research curator of the Metropolitan Museum of Art; in addition, he and his wife reviewed this catalogue carefully from the perspective of their rich heritage of Chinese culture. Carol Chang of Baltimore also assisted in the coordination of Pinyin, Wade-Giles, and the proper Chinese characters related thereto. I would be remiss if I did not mention the many hours of editing done by my friend, Mary Slusser.

It remains for me to thank the best colleague, my wife Berthe Ford, who, in addition to so much else, patiently typed the many drafts of the manuscript.

J.G.F.

Edward Choate O'Dell
1901-1982
A Memoir By John Gilmore Ford

One of the reasons why Edward O'Dell's collection of Chinese snuff bottles ranks among the very finest of this century is that when Edward wanted a bottle, Edward wanted a bottle. He didn't rest until he got it, and got it home. Back in the late Sixties he was determined to have an embellished malachite bottle (catalogue no. 59), which then belonged to the well-known collector Lilla Perry, who was also a friend. For three years he pursued the object of his desire, but every time he brought up the subject Mrs. Perry's reply was, 'I'm sorry, but there's a waiting list on that one.'

Finally Edward could stand it no longer. He decided to storm Mrs. Perry's defenses and overwhelm her. He doubled his previous offer (even the doubled offer would seem tiny compared with today's prices). Overcome, Mrs. Perry could resist no longer. She wrote (she always wrote, never phoned) and said that yes, Edward could have the bottle. Should she send it?

Oh no. The day he got the letter, Edward called her and said he would come and pick up the bottle the following day. Edward lived in Baltimore. Mrs. Perry lived in Los Angeles. The next morning I drove him to the airport, and little more than twenty-four hours after he had received the letter, he was standing in Mrs. Perry's living room with the bottle in his hands.

The next day he was back. I said to him, 'Edward, why didn't you stay out there a few days and enjoy yourself?'

'No,' he said, 'I had to bring the bottle back.' Somehow, he really didn't think it was safely his until it was home.

Like all successful collectors, Edward knew that you had to be both tenacious and untiring in the search. For hours on end he would read newspaper advertisements for sales, and if anything seemed at all interesting—if there were any Oriental objects mentioned—he got on the telephone. If he thought it sounded good, he went. One steaming summer day he dragged me up to an auction exhibition in a barn outside Westminster, Maryland. It was hot as only a country barn with one hundred and fifty people in it on a 95-degree day *can* be hot.

I had no hope that Edward was going to find anything interesting, but he poked around and finally came up with a box containing forty-five snuff bottles. Even then I didn't think much of the find, because they were all dumped into the box haphazardly, and you could see at a glance that some had chips or other flaws. I didn't think it worth the effort to go back to the sale, but Edward went, hoping that no one else would be there who wanted the box of bottles.

Well, it turned out that there was a Washington dealer there who bid Edward all the way up to $420 for the box. Edward professed a little disappointment that he had to pay so much, but he knew very well what he was doing. Among the contents was one Imperial yellow bottle with the Qianlong emperor's seal on it—worth far more alone than Edward had paid for the whole box; and there were many more which, with a little repair here or there, turned out to be fine specimens. Most amazing of all, thirty-nine of the bottles were of Imperial yellow glass (some the true emperor's yellow of the eighteenth century, others of the nineteenth). And with the exception of one pair, every one was different in size, shape, or value of color.

Edward always kept this group of yellow bottles in a case in his bedroom. I think, in addition to his love of themselves, they stood for something he told a young collector late in his life: 'Don't get weary of searching.'

Edward never got weary of searching, though snuff bottle collecting—indeed the collecting of Oriental art—was an avocation carried on in addition to his three separate careers as engineer, lawyer, and musician. It sounds pompous to call someone a Renaissance man these days, because immediately everybody thinks you are comparing him to Michelangelo; but in terms of the scope and variety of his interests, Edward was more like a fifteenth century man than like a man born to this age of specialization.

He came in with the century. He was born June 14, 1901, in a frame house which still stands on Liberty Road at Harrisonville, northwest of Baltimore. The son of Herbert F. O'Dell and Anna Mabel Choate O'Dell, he was named Edward Choate O'Dell. He was always proud to have as his middle name his mother's maiden name, for the Choates had long been figures in politics and education in New England.

When he was three, Edward was thrown from a carriage and lost an eye. You would never have known it in later life, for his sight with one eye was as keen as most people's with two. For years after the accident he wore a patch, the source of a great deal of ridicule from his schoolmates, until eventually his parents got him a glass eye.

By this time, the family was living in downtown Baltimore, and Edward was showing an extraordinary aptitude for music. At thirteen, he was made substitute organist at his church, St. Paul's Methodist on West Fayette street, though his legs were too short for him to reach the pedals.

He went to Baltimore Polytechnic Institute—known to every Baltimorean as Poly—and from there directly into the sophomore class at the Johns Hopkins University, from which he graduated in 1921 with a bachelor's degree in engineering. He was immediately appointed assistant sanitary engineer for Baltimore County. At the same time that he was designing roads and culverts (many still in use), he was pursuing both music and law. At twenty-three, he was appointed organist and choirmaster at Grace Methodist Church on Lafayette Square in West Baltimore, a position he held for twelve years. And he was going to the University of Maryland Law School at night. He graduated in 1926 and was admitted to the bar the following year.

But all this work had exhausted him, and his parents were afraid it would endanger his health. So in early 1927 they sent him on a Mediterranean cruise which included stops in the Holy Land and Egypt. The trip was his first major motivation for art collecting, and his brief glimpse of the Near East was one of the things that turned him in the direction of Oriental art.

When he returned, he gave up engineering for law and music. He practiced estate and probate law in Baltimore. He was made organist of St. Mark's Methodist Church in 1936, a post he was to hold for forty-two years. In 1943 he became organist of Har Sinai Temple as well, a position he held almost until his death. He also found time to become a 33rd degree Mason, and to be organist of both the Grand Lodge of Maryland and the Ancient and Accepted Scottish Rite of Free Masonry; altogether he played in a dozen different lodges for a total of fifty years.

It was when he was in his thirties that he began collecting Oriental art somewhat seriously. His interest, he later said, may have had its origin to some degree in his childhood, when, to play the part of a Chinese boy in a church pageant, he had to learn a hymn in Chinese. He always remembered the words of the hymn; from time to time he recited them to me—Edward reciting a hymn in Chinese was something to hear—and he believed that experience had definitely been one source of his later interest in Chinese culture.

Another influence was his trips, beginning with the cruise and going on to many later trips in this country and abroad.

By the 1930s, he was going to auctions and estate sales, mainly buying Oriental art. In 1937, at a sale at the Galton-Osborne auction house on Howard street, he spied a pair of little bottles of cinnabar lacquer. He didn't know what they were, but the material fascinated him, and he bought them for $2.50. Only later did he learn they were snuff bottles. Thus began his collection.

He bought some more bottles in 1938. Arriving in New York from a trip to Europe, he happened into the shop of Honcan Bough on Madison Avenue and selected from a prominent display of bottles the best glass, agate, and jade ones.

Though during World War II it was difficult to find good things, Edward continued to collect throughout the 1940s and 1950s. While he bought snuff bottles, in this period he was more generally interested in Oriental art and purchased in all areas including fine jades, decorative screens, and furniture. One of his prized possessions was a throne chair reputedly brought out of China during the Boxer Rebellion. He found it in the house of a Baltimore collector, and bought it for a nominal sum. Many of Edward's visitors have admired this beautifully designed piece, certainly of a late eighteenth century date, with deeply carved lacquer on wood, delicately gilded with applied medallions of cloisonné work.

He also made significant purchases at the great liquidation sale of the Yamanaka Company in New York shortly after the beginning of World War II. The company possessed major works in many areas of Oriental art, of which Edward bought some choice jades and porcelains, a six-panel screen inlaid with semi-precious stones, and additional snuff bottles.

By 1960, in addition to his other Oriental works, Edward owned about 50 snuff bottles. The appearance in that year of Lilla Perry's book, *Chinese Snuff Bottles: The Adventures and Studies of a Collector,* opened his eyes, as it did those of so many, and turned his attention to snuff bottles in particular. Mrs. Perry, who became Edward's good friend, was a person of high intelligence and a knowledgeable collector. Some scholars have criticized her book as essentially an amateur effort. There are errors in it, but if it was an amateur effort it was one in the best sense—it was by a lover of the subject whose delightful account was a major factor in the revival of interest in snuff bottle collecting.

Edward, who came upon the book quite by accident, was so excited by it that he wrote Mrs. Perry a letter, congratulating her. She wrote back, and he responded with an invitation. Not long after, on a trip to visit relatives in New England, she traveled south to see Edward's collection and that of John Ruckman of Doylestown, Pennsylvania. Edward, who went to pick her up at the train station in Baltimore, had no idea what she looked like; but when a woman got off the train wearing around her neck a magnificent jade pendant, he went up to her and said, 'You *must* be Mrs. Perry.' And so she was.

When she had been taken through Edward's entire collection of Oriental art, she said, 'Mr. O'Dell, for the lovely things you have, you must have some better bottles.' And she offered to look on the West Coast for bottles to enhance his collection.

Shortly after she got back to Los Angeles, a package arrived for Edward containing six or eight beautiful bottles, all of which he bought. The friendship and the parcels of bottles grew each month, until he had purchased seventy-five bottles from her, including fourteen which are pictured in her book. He never regretted any purchase that he made from Mrs. Perry, but once he had great regret over the outcome of a purchase.

Edward's sister, Georgia Corinne, who taught flute in the public schools, had also begun collecting snuff bottles. One of Mrs. Perry's treasures was a fine carnelian bottle carved in the form of a water buffalo with a boy on its back playing a flute. Edward was determined to have it as a present for his sister, and as always he persisted until the object was his. But Mrs. Perry was so reluctant to let it go that Edward got it only with the proviso, to which he agreed, that if at any time she regretted her decision, she could have it back.

After that particular trip to Los Angeles to pick up the bottle, Edward didn't return right away but took in some Western sights including the Grand Canyon. At some point on the trip he looked into the little box in which the bottle had been packed and found it empty. The bottle was never found. Not only was he devastated at the loss of the bottle, but it was the very one which he had agreed Mrs. Perry could have back if she wanted it. When he got home, there was nothing to do but write her and confess the loss. Someone else might have been outraged, and the friendship might have ended right there. But Mrs. Perry, as always, was understanding.

Like all collectors, Edward bought most of his bottles from well-known dealers, estates, and auctions, many of them in New York and London. He advised newcomers to buy from established collections, as he did from collections such as those of J. P. Morgan, Dwight Harris, Burton Holmes, Rodman Wanamaker, Martin Schoen, Henry J. Heinz and others. The provenance of a bottle, Edward thought, added another dimension to its interest.

He bought a number of fine bottles from a New York collector, and after the collector's death continued to buy from his daughter. It was a time when prices were going up. The collector's daughter named her price for each of the bottles she sold, and Edward gladly paid it without a word of argument. (He always either accepted the price of a bottle or didn't buy it—he never haggled.) Once he agreed to buy from the collector's daughter a finely carved coral boat for what was at the time a very high price, even though he didn't especially want it, in order to get at the same time a bottle which he very much wanted. (Later he was glad he had bought the boat, for it is a beautiful piece and has been much admired.) But despite his continuing willingness to meet her demands, the lady became suspicious that Edward was taking advantage of her. 'You got that last bottle too cheap,' she would say when we went to New York to see her. 'But I paid you what you asked,' Edward would reply. That didn't satisfy her. Eventually she became so convinced that she had been taken that she didn't want to see us anymore. Edward was sorry about that, but there was nothing he could do.

There is no doubt that he bought some

splendid bottles from her. Over the years his vision kept pace with his taste, and he developed the ability to know the best in any collection he saw. His favorites were the more decorative bottles, but he also recognized the importance of the simpler but extremely elegant ones, and bought them as well. Under his tutelage I became more and more knowledgeable, too, and in later years we often worked as a team. One of the memorable instances of this was when Edward made his largest single purchase—half of the collection of Ralph M. Hults.

Mr. Hults was a well-known West Coast collector who, partly through extremely aggressive buying tactics and partly because he was willing to pay up to double the market value for any bottle he happened to want, amassed an important collection numbering two hundred bottles in the space of ten years.

After his death in 1969, Edward wanted many of the items in his collection, but not all of them. Because of this, and because of the fact that the price asked for the collection was considered quite high, Edward sought out another leading collector and they agreed to buy the collection together and split it in the fairest possible way.

Although the collection had been offered to various people on the West Coast and all had turned it down as too expensive, by the time Edward and his colleague went to pick it up, many people there realized that they had made a mistake in not grabbing it. There were, unfortunately, some sour grapes.

The collection was brought to Edward's house in Baltimore, where all two hundred bottles were put out on the dining room table. The method of selection agreed on was this: After a full day of study, the two collectors would toss a coin. The winner of the toss got to pick the first bottle, and then the other man got to pick the next one, and so on alternating until all the bottles had been chosen and each had half the collection.

At the end of the preview day, Edward and I made a list of the bottles we wanted, in order, and decided to stick to it faithfully. If the other collector picked the bottle that was next on our list, we would go on to the following one without rethinking or trying to second guess. Edward knew exactly which bottles he wanted, and in what order.

On the day chosen for beginning the selection process, Edward won the toss. His first choice was the carved amber with the pearl (cat. no. 68), which may be the finest amber bottle in existence. The other collector, going next, took a considerable time and then selected the bottle that was third on our list. Thus at our second turn we could pick our second choice, and felt that we had got the two best bottles in the collection.

The selection process went on for three or four days, while the other collector and his wife remained Edward's guest. Since we had our list, when it came time to make our selection we just went into the dining room and picked up a bottle. But the other collector took more and more time to make his choices. Gradually he and his wife became somewhat upset, as it was increasingly evident to them (as to us) that, while they were getting some fine bottles, they were not always getting the best of the remaining bottles.

After a couple of days the wife came to me and said, as if it were somehow unfair, that we were getting the best bottles because we knew more. I offered to help them make their selections; or, if they didn't want that, I said, we could stop the selection process until they had called in any expert they liked.

Well, they decided not to take advice, and as the week wore on there was increasing tension in the house. By the time the whole business was over, they were more than ready to leave and we were more than ready to see them go. We were really afraid that a friendship had come to an end; and indeed it had been strained somewhat. But after a month or so there was communication again, and complete harmony returned to the relationship.

I have mentioned that Mrs. Perry's book started a wave of snuff bottle collecting. In a few years the interest was so great that Carl Wright, a dealer in Dallas, Texas, held an exhibition of snuff bottles, invited Mrs. Perry to speak, and asked her to invite a number of her most interested friends to attend and bring their best bottles to add to the exhibit. Edward was among those present, and took twelve bottles. That was, so far as I know, the first gathering of collectors for a public showing of bottles. In 1967, Mrs. Perry was again invited to lecture, this time at the Portland, Oregon museum. The group included many people who had been to Dallas the year before, plus others from the Northwest.

By that time Edward knew of at least one hundred people who had a more than peripheral interest in snuff bottles. Thinking that there were more that he didn't know of, and thinking of the meetings in Dallas and Portland, he came to the belief that there should be a formal organization devoted to learning about and exhibiting the little bottles which so many found so fascinating.

Many of his friends thought this was a foolish idea, and there was not much encouragement. But Edward and I decided to go ahead anyway. We incorporated The Chinese Snuff Bottle Society of America in November, 1968. Mrs.

Perry was enthusiastic, and gave us a list of the people who had written to her since the publication of her book. We sent out a letter of invitation to join, announced a quarterly newsletter, and scheduled, with some trepidation, our first convention, at The Asia Society in New York.

To our considerable surprise, one hundred and nineteen people came to that first convention. It was as though collectors had been waiting all their lives for this to happen. We were launched. Edward became the society's first president, a position he held until he died.

After that convention the society grew quickly, and our annual conventions grew larger and larger. By 1974, when we held our convention in London, there were many members from other countries. Accordingly, we decided to rename the organization The International Chinese Snuff Bottle Society. We also decided to rename our publication a journal, and to publish it in a much more sophisticated way. The society has continued to grow since then, until it now has six hundred members.

Edward, of course, attended all the conventions up through 1981, and over the years welcomed a constant stream of collectors to his home in Baltimore. Many of the annual meetings have been held there, too.

A quiet, gentle, and unassuming man, Edward was at the same time warm and friendly to all, and people quickly grew fond of him. He reciprocated not only with an affection as great as that which he lavished on his little bottles, but with a generous outpouring of knowledge and advice as well.

I remember a young collector asking him for some advice at one of the recent conventions. Edward, always encouraging, told him that he should not despair if he couldn't afford top bottles at first —there were many fine and interesting bottles at reasonable prices. 'As the years pass on,' he said, 'the novice becomes an amateur, and then an authority, and soon is equipped to improve his collection, leading to the discovery of masterpieces. Don't get weary of searching, because that is half the fun; and if you are tenacious, you will always find the bottle you are seeking.'

In recent years Edward developed a heart condition which slowed him down considerably. He gave up all of his professional organ commitments except the Masonic ones, which were the least taxing. Members who attended snuff bottle conventions of the last few years were aware of his increasing frailty, but his wit and sparkle, his enthusiasm and the radiance of his personality, were undiminished.

Last February, he spent a couple of weeks in the hospital. He came home, but continued to weaken, and died on Wednesday, March 24.

His interest in snuff bottles continued until the end, and he never got weary of searching. Shortly before he died, he asked me to put in a bid for him on a bottle to be sold at an auction on March 26. The bottle was knocked down to him, and so the last of his purchases was added to his collection two days after he died.

Snuff and Chinese Snuff Bottles:
An Historical View
by Emily Byrne Curtis

Smoking, snuffing, or chewing of various plants and herbs has been practiced from ancient times. Wherever man found suitable plants he adapted them for ritual, therapeutic, and recreational purposes. When the first Europeans came to the New World, they found two species of tobacco, *Nicotiana Tabacum* and *Nicotiana Rustica,* and while the exact original habitats of these plants are uncertain, evidence points strongly to the interior of Brazil for the former and to Mexico for the latter. As one nineteenth century traveler explained: 'Columbus first beheld smokers in the Antilles, Pizzaro found chewers in Peru, but it was in the country first discovered by Cabral that the great sternutatory was originally found. Brazilian Indians were the fathers of snuff and its best fabricators.'[1] It was in Brazil that the Portuguese learned the use of tobacco, and they were most active in the diffusion of the custom. Their influence was evident all along the routes of commerce in Africa and India. They were in Asiatic waters as early as 1511, and in 1535 the Portuguese established the first European colony in the Far East in Aomen, in the confines of China. Varieties of tobacco indigenous to Brazil are known to have reached Aomen before 1600, concurrent with the almost simultaneous introductions of tobacco to the seaports of Java and Japan. Tobacco soon found its way into China.

The Chinese were quick to deal in this new and valuable commodity and in disseminating the custom of smoking throughout the interior of Asia. Zhang Jiebin (1563-1640), a noted physician from Zhejiang, may have been the first Chinese to write on tobacco. He observed: 'only recently, during the period Wanli (1573-1619), of our Ming dynasty, it [tobacco] was cultivated in Fujian and Guangdong and from there spread into the northern provinces.'[2] Fang Yizhi (d.1667) wrote in his encyclopedia *Wu-li Xiao shi* that the *tan-ba-gu* smoke plant[3] was brought to Fujian province at the end of the Wanli period. Other Chinese writers are in general agreement and credit the Fujianese with obtaining the tobacco plant from the Philippines.

Curiously enough, the Portuguese never seemed to be mentioned in connection with tobacco. One explanation might be that the Chinese scholar class would not admit that China had anything to learn from association with the foreign barbarians and only tolerated the Portuguese presence at Aomen for reasons of commerce. With the Portuguese traders came missionaries, and where the traders established themselves along the China coast the missionaries did likewise. It is perhaps appropriate that the earliest known reference to the use of snuff in China can be found in the work of one of these men.

A Dominican priest who had volunteered for the Philippine mission, Domingo Fernandez Navarrete (1618-1686), arrived at Aomen in July of 1658. He wandered through the Southern provinces until he settled with some Dominican friars at Fu-an in Fujian. In his *Tratados Historicos,* Navarrete stated: 'Throughout the whole empire they smoke much tobacco, and so there is an abundance sowed. I have bought it for a penny a pound dry to make snuff.'[4] Navarrete's missionary activities came to an abrupt halt in 1664 when a fierce and general persecution broke out. All missionaries were to be brought to Beijing by imperial command and then conducted to Guangzhou. Morever the prohibition of maritime trade along the coastline of Guangdong was to be strictly enforced. Since Aomen was under Chinese jurisdiction, the Portuguese colony would have been subjected to martial law except for the intervention of the Jesuit, Johan Adam von Bell Schall (1591-1666), then in favor at court. While he obtained for Aomen an exemption from the regulation requiring removal inland, the regulation relating to trade and commerce remained in force. Aomen suffered greatly from this control of communication, and in 1667 Portugal decided to send an embassy to alleviate the situation. The ambassador, Manuel de Saldanha (d. 1670), did not have permission to go to Beijing immediately, nor did he bring any tribute with him. Aomen had to furnish this, and to support him, his suite, and his family which accompanied him for two years. The stranded Portuguese embassy was finally granted permission to proceed to the capital in 1670—a decision closely associated with the imperial favor enjoyed by the Jesuits. Snuff boxes and tobacco were included in the list of presents sent to Beijing,[5] and this occasion may mark the first introduction of snuff to the Manzu court.

At court, the young Kangxi emperor (1662-1722) had just attained his majority. His reign would mark a period of triumph for Western learning in China. Until the arrival of the Portuguese at the opening of the sixteenth century, China had been remote, aloof, and bound up in her own customs. As a rising threat from the Manzus in the north created an urgent need for Western cannon, the Ming court sent for the Jesuits from Aomen to cast guns. However, the Ming dynasty (1368-1644) had long passed its zenith and entered a state of decline. Taking advantage of internal rebellions, the Manzus penetrated China and ultimately established a new dynasty. In October of 1644, the Qing court moved from Shenyang to Beijing and the first emperor of the new dynasty assumed the reign title, Shunzhi (1644-1661).

Various theories have been presented as to when the court acquired the habit of taking snuff. Some are based on the supposition of prior Manzu knowledge, since it is generally held that tobacco was introduced into Manchuria by the Koreans, who had adopted it from Japan. While there are certainly references to the Manzus eating tobacco,[6] there is no mention of them taking snuff—a preparation of powdered tobacco taken up into the nose by sniffing. Neither the Japanese nor the Koreans used snuff. Indeed, there has yet to surface a single reference to snuff in all records, written by merchants and missionaries alike, sent from Japan in the sixteenth and seventeenth centuries. Twice a year the Koreans sent a tribute mission to Beijing. Among their gifts was a finely shredded tobacco which the Chinese preferred to their own product; snuff is not mentioned.

Martino Martini (1614-1661), a Jesuit priest, was in Beijing at the time of its occupation by the Manzus. He noted: 'At their girdle there hangs on either side two handkerchiefs to wipe their face and hands; besides, there hangs a knife for all necessary uses, with two purses, in which they carry tobacco or such like commodities.'[7] A member of the Dutch embassy of 1651 made a similar observation: 'At their sides hangeth a knife and two little Purses, wherein they put Tobacco, which is taken by them with great delight, insomuch that the Noblest Visitants are treated with the same, it being brought to them lighted by the Servant of the House.'[8] Perhaps the most conclusive piece of evidence comes from Father Jean Grueber, S. J. (1628-1680). An acute observer and trained mathematician who had access to court circles, he reported: 'They take no tobacco in powder, but in smoke: the "Tartars" and the "Chinese", the men and the women are great takers of tobacco...'[9]

Although snuff does not appear to have been in use at the court during this period, it was present in the southern, coastal provinces. Unlike smoking, which was initially denounced, snuff first gained official acceptance as a curative. Missionaries, particularly the Jesuits, used snuff and their role in its introduction into China cannot be easily discounted. One of the six master painters of early Qing dynasty, Wu Li (Simon Xavier a Cunha, 1623-1718), entered the novitiate of the Society of Jesus at Aomen in 1682. He described his life in Aomen during this period in a collection of poems which he entitled *San-ba ji*, in reference to St. Paul's (São Paulo) cathedral where he had studied. A poem written in 1684 gives thanks to a friend for giving him snuff to cure his sickness.

> Unsatisfied gluttony brings endless sickness;
> Searching everywhere for a good prescription
> I find a distant friend.
> It is not known that this kind of tobacco can cure a sickness;
> However, it makes my nostrils also greedy for more.[10]

Later, Wu Li began to make snuff himself. The remainder of his life was devoted to missionary work in Nanjing and Shanghai.

In keeping with his desire to have personal contact with the people, the Kangxi emperor made tours of the southern provinces. He could also keep in contact with the missionaries in the central provinces and thus keep relations at an informal level, rendering formal recognition of their status unnecessary. During his tour of 1684, the Kangxi emperor visited Nanjing. He was welcomed, by, among others, the Jesuit Fathers Jean Valat (1599-1696), and Jean-Dominique Gabiani (1623-1696), who presented gifts. According to a Chinese source, the *Xi-zhao Ding-an*, the Emperor kept one and returned the others. This one was snuff.

There was a considerable traffic of gifts from the missionaries, mainly of wine and Western medicines. The Jesuits also engaged in commerce and they were severely criticized for this practice; particularly for their trade in wine, tobacco, and other items.[11] Given then the fact that the Jesuits not only used snuff, but distributed it as gifts, it is reasonable to assume that they also dealt in it. On the threshold of the eighteenth century, the Jesuits noticed that no present was more acceptable to the court of Beijing than snuff from Brazil, which came from Aomen, via Lisbon, Goa, and Malacca. Apparently, the court still regarded snuff as a medicinal aid, for in 1693, Ysbrants Ides, a member of the Russian embassy, mentioned that during a banquet: 'The Viceroy and other Lords diverted themselves by smoking Tobacco.'[12] The trend, however, was changing.

Wang Hao (*Jinshi* 1703) in his *Sui luan ji en* left this bright entry for August 17, 1703:

> On this day the heir apparent made a present of one glass snuff bottle. The tobacco plant is produced abroad on the island of Chang-ch'i [Nagasaki, Japan]. Europeans mix it with an aromatic substance and carry it in bottles at their belts. One takes a portion of it on one's little finger and places it in both nostrils. The fragrance clears the brain and is specially able to drive away disease.[13]

In the same year the Kangxi emperor's favorite personal secretary, Gao Shiji (1645-1703), retired. According to *Peng-shan miji* Gao's account of his visit to the Palace, the Emperor took from his own belt two snuff bottles which he used himself and one bottle of snuff to give to his servant. Afterwards a gift of four snuff bottles and one jar of snuff was bestowed upon him.[14]

We see therefore, at the turn of the seventeenth century, an increasing number of references to the exchange and use of snuff in the Manzu court, and that, supported by imperial patronage, snuff-taking began to develop into a fashionable habit with its own ritual. For a snuff container the Chinese simply adapted something already in use, small bottles for drugs and medicines; later, original snuff bottles would be fashioned of every conceivable material.[15] It is noteworthy that the Europeans in China are mentioned as also carrying snuff in bottles. Westerners normally carried snuff in boxes, but in the humid climate of the Far East the bottle provided a more suitable container.

At another audience, the Kangxi emperor had shown Gao Shiji new articles of glassware declaring that China's product was now superior to that produced in the West. Glass, though known by the Chinese during the Zhou dynasty (1122-254 B.C.), was not utilized significantly until the Europeans reintroduced it to China in the eighteenth century. The Emperor had established workshops for research into the arts and sciences and the glass atelier was under the direction of the German Jesuit Bernard-Kilian Stumpf (1655-1720). Wang Shizhen (1634-1711), listed, in 1705, glass snuff bottles from the palace workshops as having been made in every shape, and in six colors; red, purple, yellow, white, black, and green.[16]

French Jesuits had brought enamel paintings and enamel wares as part of the rich presents to the Kangxi emperor from Louis XIV in 1688, and expertise at producing them was added to their other skills. In 1713, the Emperor celebrated his sixtieth birthday. Catalogued in the list of presents made to the sovereign on this occasion were two bottles of snuff, as the gifts of the Jesuits. Three snuff bottles, enameled in the Western style, and two bottles filled with snuff were presented by a wealthy Chinese courtier Wang Hongxu (1645-1723), who had just been restored to imperial favor.[17]

A veritable craze for enamel wares developed. Not only were enamel wares produced for official households, but by the Qianlong (1736-1795) period, they were being manufactured for daily use by the common people. This art form, although it originated in the West, was thoroughly mastered by the Chinese artist. The book, *Yangzhou huafang lu*, tells us of one famous enamel artist, Wang Shixiong, who lived during the Yongzheng (1723-1735) and Qianlong periods.

> ...he had many friends, and his fame spread throughout the land. In the capital his fine craftsmanship was praised, this artist being known in Peking as the enamel ware King.[18]

Finely decorated snuff bottles of the most exquisite quality were among the articles manufactured and these snuff bottles certainly rank with, and may be, THE masterpieces of enamel painting in China.

Jesuits toiled daily in the palace workshops painting, engraving, or repairing mechanical devices, and Jesuit physicians even attended the Kangxi emperor. Unfortunately, the Jesuits' success at court had aroused the jealousy of the Franciscan and Dominican missionaries. These missionaries, who had arrived in China later than the Jesuits, found their works overshadowed by those of the Jesuits. They accused the Jesuits of compromising the integrity of the Roman Catholic faith and misleading the Christians in China. A controversy erupted, and in 1705 the Pope had to send a legate, Charles Thomas Maillard de Tournon (1668-1710), to China. During the entertainment at the New Year's Festival of 1706, the Kangxi emperor sent de Tournon some refreshment, and gave him a crystal snuff bottle—which may be the first recorded instance of a Chinese snuff bottle traveling to the West.[19] And so, here again, we have the ever-pervasive snuff bottle present in the background of historical events.

During the eighteenth century, the volume of European trade with China, all of it through Guangzhou, rose steadily. Aomen became in effect the outpost of all Western trade in China—indeed the center, and fulcrum of foreign relations —an exclusive position she maintained until the opening of other treaty ports to foreign residence in 1841. The Jesuits in Beijing often obtained exemptions for Aomen to Chinese regulations relating to trade and commerce. In return for this favored status, the Portuguese at Aomen paid an annual ground rent which was usually sent to Beijing with elaborate presents. In 1714, Father Kilian Stumpf presented to the Kangxi emperor forty-eight small bottles of 'tabaco de amostrinha'—a fine snuff from Brazil —as a part of the gifts from the Senate of Aomen. The tribute for 1721 contained snuff of the first grade called fei-yan, and that of the second grade, dou-yan, snuff of a duck green color.[20] Tobacco was a Portuguese state monopoly and to meet the increasing demand Lisbon had in 1719 granted Aomen the privilege of receiving from Brazil two ships annually with cargoes of snuff. This trade, administered from the Portuguese colony of Goa, continued until the end of the eighteenth century, when the Portuguese shipping at Aomen dwindled to just the consignment of snuff from Brazil.

Various embassies also presented snuff bottles and boxes to the Manzu court. Rome was most anxious to establish diplomatic relations with Beijing, and after de Tournon's unsuccessful attempt resolved to send another mission. The *Guangdong Provincial Gazette* for 1731[21] recorded the arrival of the papal legate, Carlo Ambrogio Mezzabarba (c. 1685-1741), in 1720. While he brought '2 small cases of snuff, each containing 6 canisters,' to the Kangxi emperor, the Pope's gifts to the succeeding Yongzheng emperor in 1725 included: '11 ivory embedded snuff boxes; a pair of snuff cannisters and playthings such as snuff bottles,'[22] made from a wide variety of materials. Not to be outdone, the Portuguese ambassador, Alexandre Metello de Sousa e Menezes, in 1727 offered carved crystal bottles with *amostrinha* and snuff boxes from Paris and London. Francisco de Assis Pacheco de Sampaio, who headed the Portuguese embassy in 1752, (during the Qianlong period), gave *amostrinha* and very elaborate snuff boxes fashioned from gold, mother-of-pearl, agate, and enamel. Among the presents from the Qianlong emperor to the ambassador was a molded gourd snuff bottle.[23]

It is not to be supposed that all of this activity was confined to the court at Beijing. As has been mentioned earlier, not only was snuff in use by missionaries and traders of the south, in late seventeenth century China, but the great ports of Guangzhou and Aomen at that time served as transfer points for all tributes and gifts, including snuff, destined for the court. As early as 1710, Li Xu (1655-1729), the textile commissioner at Suzhou, Jiangsu Province, recorded sending 'brushes from Chekiang, snuff bottles, and jars for bird seed,'[24] to the Kangxi emperor. The *Guangdong Gazette* mentioned above recorded the various embassies as they passed through Guangzhou—a great center of manufacture. Lovely enamel snuff bottles were decorated there; occasionally even one with a Western, or Christian motif on it.[25] The famous porcelain kilns at Jingdezhen, Jiangxi, produced snuff bottles for local use, the court, and export to the West.[26] *A History of Aomen, Aomen jilu,* prepared in the first part of the eighteenth century describes how the Portuguese there had little purses which they carried upon themselves for snuff bottles.[27] At Kiakhta, trade in 'Portuguese snuff in Chinese form,'[28] was common enough to be mentioned in passing by various witnesses and Earl Macartney's (1737-1806) account of his travels through China to Beijing in 1793 even included the observation: 'They also take snuff, mostly Brazil...'[29] It certainly seemed as if everyone in China used snuff, and it is tempting to credit Aomen with creating the demand for snuff bottles. By the late eighteenth century, the snuff bottle was common enough to appear in typical reverse glass paintings made expressly for export to the West.[30] At the same time, the West was busily supplying the mandarins connected with foreign trade with 'sing-songs' —mechanical devices—such as snuff boxes with birds that popped up from the inside when the box was opened, and sang a little song. In one macabre episode, a viceroy of Guangzhou (Jiqing, d. 1802), committed suicide by swallowing 'his stone snuff bottle.'[31]

The volume of Western trade through Guangzhou continued to rise steadily throughout the nineteenth century and consignments of snuff were included in the cargos of ships from England, France, and Sweden.[32] Under William Milburn's list of 'Articles procurable at Canton, with directions on how to use them' are '... Blood Coloured Agate. [It] is more beautiful than most of this class.... The stone is much esteemed when well marked, and is chiefly used for the tops of snuff boxes. The Blackish veined Brown Agate is found in pieces that have a pretty smooth surface.... It is capable of a very beautiful polish, and is commonly cut into seals, buttons, heads of canes, and the tops of snuff boxes.' Pieces of opal 'in size that of a walnut' were also available.[33] Gold snuff boxes were among the items imported in 1803;[34] in 1849, British officials used one in lieu of payment of rent;[35] while in 1860 Franco-British troops found gold snuff boxes during the looting of the Summer Palace.[36]

All transactions pertaining to foreign trade were handled by a group of government appointed traders known as hong merchants, a number of whom attained great prominence and had their portraits painted—in Western style oils—which sometimes show them holding a snuff bottle.[37] A more traditional Chinese painting depicts Qi-ying (d. 1858), the imperial commissioner at Guangzhou (1842), with a snuff bottle.[38] Add to this two portraits of the Daoguang emperor (1821-1850)[39] with snuff bottles and it can be safely stated that the heyday of snuff-taking had truly arrived.

Chinese artisans lavished their unsurpassed craftsmanship and technical expertise on the production of snuff bottles. Glass, once only produced within the Forbidden City, was now made at Boshan in Shandong province. Splendid agate and jade snuff bottles were carved at workshops in Suzhou, Jiangsu province. Yixing ware, named for a district west of Shanghai, and highly esteemed by both Chinese and Japanese collectors, was easily adapted to containers for snuff. It was the era for exotic materials; coconut shell, bamboo, sharkskin, pearl, aquamarine, tourmaline, and hornbill ivory. Superb quality bottles, presumably for the Chinese market, were manufactured in Japan. To this list must be added the development of another southern innovation, the inside-painted bottle. Sometime in the early nineteenth century, a painter conceived the idea of putting his pictures inside snuff bottles, with the advantage of protecting his work from wear, and adding a novelty value to it. Inside-painted snuff bottles illustrate two traditional forms of Chinese art—painting and calligraphy—and were cherished as such by a number of Chinese scholar collectors.[40]

While the earliest known dated example of an inside-painted bottle is 1816,[41] evidence exists to suggest an earlier date for the initial development of the art form.[42] From the early 1880's on, however, the greatest production of inside-painted bottles was centered in Beijing—a practice which has continued to this day. The field was dominated by three artists beginning with Zhou Leyuan, perhaps the greatest of these, the prolific Ye Zhongsan, and Ma Shaoxuan, who painted a remarkable series of portrait bottles depicting the leading political figures of the time.[43] Works by Ding Erzhong were especially valued by Chinese collectors since he was from the scholar class and thus considered a non-commercial artist.[44]

As the habit of snuffing gained in popularity, good snuff bottles became the subject of active acquisition and collection by court officials. In the last years of the Qianlong reign, two viceroys of Fujian were found guilty of corruption and lists of spoils confiscated included a considerable number of snuff bottles.[45] At the beginning of the Jiaqing reign (1796-1820), the great mandarin Heshen (1750-1799) was arrested and a remarkably large number of snuff bottles were found in his household.[46] Later, the first Prince Cheng, Yongxing (1752-1823) was given part of Heshen's garden near the Summer Palace. He stored a large collection of books and objects of art in a studio called Yijinzhai. Several snuff bottles are known which bear this studio name.[47] The mark Xing-you heng-tang, 'The Hall of Constancy,' which belonged to Zaiquan (d. 1854), the fifth Prince Ting, appears on one snuff bottle precisely dated to the jiyou year (1849) of the Daoguang emperor.[48]

The first known Chinese book on snuff and snuff bottles was not written until 1869, during the reign of the Tongzhi emperor (1862-75). Zhao Zhiqian (1829-1884) made a study of the subject, and in his treatise entitled Yong-lu xian-jie (Leisure Enquiries into Snuff), attempted an account of the use of snuff in China, of its properties, and of the ornate bottles that were made to hold it. His work was later incorporated into the Bi-yan cong-ke, along with three other essays on the same topic.[49]

Although Europeans had been trading with the Chinese since the establishment of the Portuguese settlement at Aomen, America did not enter the China trade until 1785. Enterprising traders and shipowners quickly moved in on this promising market and on December 18, 1787 a tiny eighty-ton sloop, the Experiment, left New York for Guangzhou. Her main cargo was ginseng root but also stowed in the hold were 'four casks of the best Scotch snuff.'[50] A newly independent United States of America was asserting her right to a share in the lucrative China trade. This spirit so fascinated a Dutch country-gentleman, A. E. Van Braam Houckgeest (1739-1801) that he emigrated to South Carolina. He had been connected with the Dutch trade at Guangzhou and Aomen from 1759-73. In 1784, he became a naturalized citizen of the United States. He was a friend of George Washington and Benjamin

Franklin and served as the earliest president of the American Philosophical Society. After a series of misfortunes, he returned to Guangzhou in 1790 as head of the Dutch factory.

Four years later, Houckgeest accompanied the Dutch ambassador, Issac Titsingh (1745-1811), on his embassy to Beijing. When he returned to the United States from China, he brought a large collection of Chinese art objects and presented a set of china to Martha Washington. He acquired a country house near Bristol, Pennsylvania, which he called 'China's retreat.' In 1797-98, Houckgeest published in French a two-volume work[51] on the Dutch embassy to Beijing, which he dedicated to George Washington and printed at Philadelphia. He relates that at the end of the interview, the Qianlong emperor distributed gifts consisting of small tobacco pouches and small glass bottles for snuff, while the Embassy presented gold and amber snuff boxes, and snuff from Brazil.[52] Houckgeest was regarded as a romantic figure because he was the first American who had appeared at the Celestial Court.

A large collection of Chinese objects formed by Nathan Dunn (1782-1844) during his long residence as a merchant in China was mounted in Philadelphia in 1839. The catalogue included the following items:

> 568. Richly carved ivory case, to contain a gentleman's snuff bottle.
>
> 603. Ornamental stand, with marble top, on which is a plate of wax fruit, and several coloured glass snuff bottles.
>
> 695. Porcelain snuff bottle, of great beauty, with a stopper of red cornelian, attached to which is a tortise-shell spoon.[53]

The Chinese Museum in the Marlboro Chapel, Boston, in 1845 showed an extensive collection of articles gathered by one of the attachés of the American Embassy to China (1844), and by American missionaries.[54] This entire collection was subsequently leased by P.T. Barnum (1810-1891) and exhibited in his Chinese Museum in New York City in 1850. With characteristic flair, Mr. Barnum 'secured and attached to it, regardless of the expense, the celebrated Chinese Beauty, Miss Pwan-ye-koo,' in order 'to increase its attraction, and invest its picturesque still-life with a living interest.' Included among the 'still-life' items were enameled tobacco boxes, a snuff bottle in the form of the citron or hand fruit, a very finely carved ivory case for a snuff bottle, and a number of snuff bottles of different patterns and made of different materials.[55]

Catalogued in the American Art Association's auction of April 16, 1892 was a collection of 221 snuff bottles formed by Mrs. M. J. Morgan. Composed mostly of hardstone specimens, the collection included snuff bottles which were formerly the property of Comte de Semalle, a member of the French legation at Beijing (1873-1885).[56] George A. Hearn (1835-1913), for many years secretary of legation and acting minister in Beijing, published a catalogue of his collection in 1894. He listed examples in a wide variety of materials, such as this entry for item 1060:

> Snuff-bottle of Soo Chow cinnabar lacquer. Finely carved with trees and figures on either side, the under carving showing dark olive and buff color.[57]

Some of the collections were given to museums. One of the earliest bequests went to the Metropolitan Museum of Art in 1879.[58] Dr. Berthold Laufer (1874-1934) in 1913 catalogued the collection of Mrs. George T. Smith for the Field Museum of Natural History, Chicago.[59] The acquisitive American collectors' interest in Chinese snuff bottles waned until the advent, in 1960, of Lilla S. Perry's (1882-1971), *Chinese Snuff Bottles: The Adventures and Studies of a Collector*. This delightful book has long been regarded as the snuff bottle Bible, and many collectors identify themselves as of the 'pre' or 'post' Perry era. Her book can be considered as the catalyst for the renewed interest in Chinese snuff bottles, and the inspiration for many present-day collections, perhaps best exemplified by that of Edward Choate O'Dell.

Notes

[1] Ewbank Thomas, *Life in Brazil*, New York, 1856, p. 125.

[2] Berthold Laufer, *Tobacco and Its Use in Asia*, Field Museum of Natural History, Department of Anthropology, Chicago, 1924, Leaflet number 18, p. 3.

[3] This encyclopedia on miscellaneous subjects was printed in 1664. See zhuan 9, p. 23b.

[4] Fra Domingo Fernandez Navarrete, *Tratados historicas, politicos, ethicos, y religiosos de la Monarchia de China*, 2 vols., Madrid, 1676. Original text reads: 'De otras cosas a y en la China: tabacco, en todo el Reyno se usa mucho en humo; y assi se siembra en abundancia a dos quatros he comprado la libra seco, para hazerlo polvos.' Chapter 5, C5b, p. 34. Translation from English edition of 1704.

[5] Francisco Piementel, *Breve relacao de jornada que fez a corte Pekin o senhor Manoel de Saldanha*, compiled and annotated by C. R. Boxer and J. M. Braga. Macau, 1942 pp. vii, viii. See also *Arquivos de Macau*, Imprensa Nacional, editor P.M. Sarmento, 1941, 2nd series, Vol. 1, pp. 25 et seg. I am

indebted to Charles Ralph Boxer for this reference.

[6] L. Carrington Goodrich, 'Early Prohibitions of Tobacco in China and Manchuria,' *Journal of the American Oriental Society*, Vol. 58, 1938, pp. 648-57.

[7] Martino Martini, *Bellum Tartarium, The Conquest of the Great Renowned Empire of China by the Invasion of the Tartars*, London, 1655, p. 262.

[8] John Nieuhoff (1618-1672), *An Embassy from the East India Company of the United Provinces to the Grand Tartar Cham, Emperor China*, translated by John Ogilby, London, 1669, p. 286.

[9] M. Melchisedec Thevenot, *Relations de Divers Voyages Curieux*, Paris, 1676, p. 17. 'Pour du tabac, ils n'en prennent point en poudre, mais beaucoup en fumée, aussi bien les Tartares comme les Chinois, tant les femmes que les hommes.' Father Grueber resided in China from 1660 to 1663.

[10] Gerard C. C. Tsang, 'Chinese Views on Snuff,' *Chinese Snuff Bottles*, Hong Kong Museum of Art, Oct.-Nov. 1977, p. 17.

[11] For comments on the Jesuits' commercial activities in China see *Memorie Storiche*, Ed. Cardinal Domenico Passionei, Venice, 1761, vol. 2, pp. 45-8. I am indebted to Father Antonio Sisto Rosso for this reference.

[12] Ysbrants Ides, *Three Years Travels from Moscow Overland to China*, London, 1705, p. 68.

[13] L. Carrington Goodrich, 'Snuff in China', *China*, Feb. 1942, p. 12. 'Sui luan ji en', by Wang Hao in the *Xiao-fang-hu-zhai Yu-ti Cong-chao* edition, by Wang Xiqi, 1877-78.

[14] The *Gu-xue Hui-kan* edition, compiled by Teng Shih, Shanghai n.d. Translation based on Lo-shu Fu, *A Documentary Chronicle of Sino-Western Relations (1644-1820)*, Tucson, 1966, Vol. 1, p. 113.

[15] Glass was one of the earliest materials used.

[16] *Xiang-zu Bi-ji*, 1705, zhuan 7, p. 9b.

[17] For a complete list of the presents given to the Kangxi emperor, see *Wanshou Shengdian Chu-ji*, 120 zhuan, printed during the years 1716-17.

[18] *Masterpieces of Chinese Enamel Ware in the National Palace Museum*, Taipei, 1971, pp. 64 and 128.

[19] Antonio Sisto Rosso, *Apostolic Legations to China of the Eighteenth Century*, South Pasadena, 1948, p. 163, note 35.

[20] Yin Guangren and Zhang Rulin, *Aomen jilu*. First edition 1751. Reprinted in 1890, zhuan 2, pp. 29a and 29b.

[21] Hao Yulin, *Guangdong Tongzhi*, 1731, zhuan 58, pp. 13b, 14a. Translation by Chu Kuang-fu, Oriental Division, New York Public Library.

[22] *Ibid*.

[23] Francisco de Assis Pacheco de Sampaio, *Memoria Sobre O Estabelecimento de Macau*, Lisbon, 1879, pp. 102-105.

[24] See Hong Kong Museum of Art, catalogue of the exhibition: *Snuff Bottles of the Ch'ing Dynasty*, Oct. 1978, p. 40, note 7.

[25] For a discussion of this subject, see 'Christian Motifs in Chinese Snuff Bottles', *Arts of Asia*, Jan.-Feb. 1982, pp. 82-89, by this author.

[26] See 'Chinese Snuff Bottles in the China Trade', *Arts of Asia*, March-April 1980, pp. 90-99, by this author.

[27] See note 20, zhuan 2, p. 15b.

[28] Clifford M. Foust, *Muscovite and Mandarin*, University of North Carolina Press, 1969, p. 353.

[29] J.L. Cranmer-Byng, ed., *An Embassy to China*, Hamden, Conn., 1963, p. 225.

[30] See note 26.

[31] John Barrow, *Travels in China*, London, 1804, p. 179. Also Arthur W. Hummel, ed., *Eminent Chinese of the Ch'ing Period*, United States Government Printing Office, Wash., 1943, pp. 584-85.

[32] Louis Dermigny, *Les Memoires de Charles de Constant sur le Commerce à la Chine*, Paris, 1964, p. 299.

[33] William Milburn, *Oriental Commerce*, London, 1813, pp. 497-8.

[34] See note 32, pp. 308-311.

[35] See 'The Impact of the West-Part One-China in the Nineteenth Century', by this author, *Journal of The International Chinese Snuff Bottle Society*, June 1981, pp. 7-8.

[36] Cecile and Michel Beurdeley, *Giuseppe Castiglione*, Rutland, Vermont, 1971, p. 74.

[37] See note 26, p. 91; note 35, p. 7, fig. 7.

[38] See note 35, p. 9, figs. 15-16.

[39] H.M. Moss, 'An Imperial Habit-Part Two', *Journal of The International Chinese Snuff Bottle Society*, March 1976, p. 17, figs. 91-94.

[40] Schuyler Cammann, 'Chinese Inside-Painted Snuff Bottles and their Makers', *Harvard Journal of Asiatic Studies*, Vol. 20, June 1957, pp. 295-326.

[41] A.O. Blishen, 'Early Inside Painted Snuff Bottles by Kan Huan-wen', *Journal of The International Chinese Snuff Bottle Society*, Dec. 1974, pp. 12-22.

[42] Victor E. Graham, 'Chinese Snuff Bottles: The French Connection', *Journal of The International Chinese Snuff Bottle Society*, Dec. 1979, pp. 9 and 13.

[43] See *Reflected Glory in a Bottle: Chinese Snuff Bottle Portraits*, by this author, New York, 1980.

[44] For a discussion of these artists see note 40.

[45] See note 10, p. 17.

[46] For a discussion of Heshen, see note 10, p. 17. Also 'Enamel-Painted Snuff Bottles of the Ch'ing Dynasty', Linsheng Chang, *Journal of The International Chinese Snuff Bottle Society*, March 1979, pp. 8-9.

[47] For illustrated examples, see note 24, p. 61, fig. 44, and p. 73, fig. 81.

[48] In collection of author. For examples, see note 24, p. 71, #74, and p. 105, #176.

[49] For a discussion and partial translation of these essays, see 'Chinese Snuff Bottles as Viewed by Some Old Chinese Scholars', by Schuyler Cammann, *Journal of The International Chinese Snuff Bottle Society*, June 1980, pp. 4-7, and December 1980, pp. 10-12.

[50] *Experiment, Sloop Papers, 1785-87*, (micro-film), New York Historical Society.

[51] A.E. van Braam Houckgeest, *Voyage de L'Ambassade de la Compagnie des Indes Orientales Hollandaises 1794-95*, Philadelphia, 1797.

[52] Ibid, pp. 377-79.

[53] *A Descriptive Catalogue of the Chinese Collection in Philadelphia*, Philadelphia, Printed for the Proprietor, 1839.

[54] John R. Peters, Jr., *Guide to, or Descriptive Catalogue of the Chinese Museum in the Marlboro Chapel, Boston*, Boston, 1845.

[55] *Ten Thousand Things on China and the Chinese*, New York: J.S. Renfield, Printer, 1850.

[56] *Catalogue of the Collections of the American Art Association*, New York, 1892, p. 209, #1078.

[57] *Ancient Chinese Porcelains and Other Curios*, descriptions by Hon. Chester Holocombe, New York, 1894. For cinnabar lacquer snuff bottle, see p. 172, #1060.

[58] Samuel Putnam Avery (1847-1920).

[59] Berthold Laufer, *Catalogue of a Collection of Ancient Chinese Snuff-Bottles*, Chicago, Privately Printed, 1913.

Catalogue of the Exhibition

Description

■ **1. NEPHRITE 1650-1750**—Examples of jet black jade carved with utmost simplicity in a flask shape are rare indeed. The onion-skin inclusion on one face is carved in high relief depicting a bold eagle on a large rock. The color of the material, the feel of the surface related to hundreds of years of handling, the style of the carving, the wide mouth with concave top, as well as the deep hollowing of the interior help assign this bottle to the earliest period. Height: 2 9/16 in. (6.4 cm)
Formerly in the collection of Lilla S. Perry.
Illustrated: Lilla S. Perry, *Chinese Snuff Bottles: The Adventures & Studies of a Collector*. Tuttle, Rutland, Vermont, and Tokyo, 1960, p. 105, no. 86.
Subsequently referred to as: Perry.
Illustrated: John Ford, 'Edward O'Dell's Collection,' *Arts of Asia*, Nov.-Dec. 1976, col. pl., p. 35. Subsequently referred to as: *Arts of Asia*.

■ **2. NEPHRITE 1720-1800**—The Suzhou school represents a distinct community of artisans still thriving today. Jades, agates, and other hardstones have been carved there with utmost dexterity over a period of three hundred years. This fine example of the Suzhou school of carving is rendered in an even off-white tone with subtle amber colored markings used by the artist to create shadows and highlights. One face illustrates a sage in a rocky grotto before a table with utensils. The reverse side shows a monkey fondling a fungus *lingzhi* in a similar rocky grotto. The vessel is well hollowed and reflects the early school of carving with its subtle details. Height: 2 5/8 in. (6.6 cm)
See reverse illustration on page 75.

■ **3. NEPHRITE 1750-1825**—One face of this black, gray to off-white jade is carved to illustrate the metamorphosis of the carp into the dragon. According to legend, the Yellow River carps which succeed in leaping over the Longmen (Dragon Gate) rapids turn into dragons. This motif is used to refer to students who pass their examinations with distinction and is an allusion to literary and official success. The dexterity of the artist is conveyed by the intensity of the scene, with swirling waters enveloping the central figures. The bottle is well hollowed and has a rimmed foot. In this instance the stopper, which may not be original, bears mentioning as it is an unusually fine example of a dragon relating perfectly to the theme of the bottle. Height: 2 7/16 in. (6.2 cm)
Illustrated: *Arts of Asia*, op. cit., p. 32.
Illustrated: *Journal of the International Chinese Snuff Bottle Society*, September 1977, p. 3, fig. 2. Subsequently referred to as: *JICSBS*.

■ **4. JADEITE 1800-1900**—This simple vase form of bright red to russet coloring is dramatized by high relief carving in an off-white tone of a lizard gracefully climbing the lower part of the vase with a spider above it. The reverse side illustrates a pair of grasshoppers. Height: 2 1/4 in. (5.8 cm)

■ **5. NEPHRITE 1600-1700**—The large carp design carved in gray jade with a russet colored lotus flower on one side is stylistically related to sixteenth and seventeenth century Ming carvings. It is not likely that this particular piece was fashioned originally as a snuff bottle because the mouth is not simply a drilling (that could have taken place later) but an integral part of the design, with the lips of the fish open to receive food. The vessel is probably a Ming medicine flask later adapted as a snuff bottle. Length: 4 5/8 in. (11.9 cm)
Illustrated: Bob C. Stevens, *The Collector's Book of Snuff Bottles*. Weatherhill, New York and Tokyo, 1976, no. 412. Subsequently referred to as: Stevens.

■ **6. NEPHRITE 1800-1900**—Small bottles of rounded rectangular form are common, but it is rare to find the yellow color with russet markings. The carving of prunus blossoms and branches relate effectively with the color tonalities in the jade. The plum or prunus blossom is the flower of winter but often blooms while snow is still on the ground; therefore, the poets have romantically extended the symbol to early spring. Height: 2 1/16 in. (5.3 cm)

■ **7. JADEITE 1780-1880**—A Suzhou carving rendered in gray to off-white jade illustrates an old gentleman leading a horse in a rocky landscape with pine branches above. The reverse shows a Daoist immortal performing magic with a sorcerer's fly whisk, and a dragon miraculously appearing out of the clouds. The artist again has used consummate skill in the use of dark and light areas to dramatize a mythical scene. Height: 2 5/8 in. (6.5 cm)
Illustrated: *Newsletter of the Chinese Snuff Bottle Society of America*, December 1972, p. 19, fig. 16. Subsequently referred to as: *Newsletter*.

■ **8. JADEITE 1780-1850**—The opaque dark green jadeite is frequently confused with chloromelanite but the distinguishing characteristics are the difference in the texture of the material as well as the white inclusions that can only be seen in jadeite. This flattened vase form has three sections on each side with vertical ribs delineating panels in which three archaic dragons, *chilong*, rhythmically climb the sides of the vessel. A distinctive feature of the bottle is the original stopper, which perfectly coordinates with the rest of the design. Height: 2 11/16 in. (6.8 cm)

■ **9. NEPHRITE 1725-1800**—One face of this vessel of russet and yellow green shows a man and attendant in a boat near a rocky shoreline with a pine tree hovering above. The reverse side illustrates two pairs of archaic dragons, one pair clasping the flaming pearl while the others have their heads in opposite directions, carved in relief of stylized design within a medallion. The sides reveal the typical *taotie* masks with rings in their mouths. The carver has made dramatic use of the dark areas to define the scene. Height: 2 5/8 in. (6.5 cm)
See reverse illustration on page 75.

Description

■ **10. JADEITE 1750-1825**—A pure white or mutton-fat carving, in a double gourd shape, is finely detailed with branches and foliage wrapped around the entire vessel. Miniature gourds are interspersed to echo the overall design. In the lower corner we see a restive Buddhist lion. Height: 2 1/2 in. (6.3 cm)

■ **11. JADEITE 1775-1875**—The term *feicui* has traditionally been used by the Chinese to describe gem quality jade. Originally introduced into China in the late eighteenth century, *feicui* was first imported from Burma into Yunnan Province. During the twentieth century, however, jadeite has been imported into China from all over the world, including the United States. Classic bottle form characterizes this simple vessel. Devoid of decoration except for the lavender mauve coloring, the bottle is a fine example of *feicui* jade. Height: 2 1/16 in. (5.2 cm)

■ **12. JADEITE 1790-1880**—There can be as many snuff bottle shapes as there are materials available. This ovoid jade is of a light green color with brilliant emerald green inclusions running through the bottle as well as the original matching stopper. The vessel is undecorated except for the fine abstract markings revealed by the artisan who carved the bottle. Height: 2 in. (5.1 cm)
Illustrated: *Newsletter*, December 1972, p. 19, fig. 17.

■ **13. JADEITE 1780-1880**—Since ancient times, elephants have been among the most fascinating animals to Chinese artists. This unusual white jade with high rimmed foot is supporting four elephants acting as a base for the upper section of four elephant heads with separate rings held by their trunks. An ingeniously carved matching stopper is surmounted by a small elephant depicted in the round. Height: 2 9/16 in. (6.5 cm)
Formerly in the collection of Martin Schoen.
Exhibited: China Institute in America, December 1, 1952-January 31, 1953. Catalogue of the *Exhibition of Chinese Snuff Bottles of the Seventeenth and Eighteenth Centuries from the Collection of Mr. and Mrs. Martin Schoen*, no. 4. Subsequently referred to as: China Institute. Catalogue.
Illustrated: Stevens, *op. cit.*, no. 430.

■ **14. JADEITE 1780-1880**—A famous theme in Chinese poetry speaks of the melting snows in spring. The artist of this simple rounded rectangular form brilliantly used emerald green markings on a snowy ground to illustrate the story. Height: 2 9/16 in. (6.5 cm)
Formerly in the collection of Martin Schoen.
Exhibited: China Institute. Catalogue, no. 9.
Illustrated: Stevens, *op. cit.*, no. 457.

■ **15. NEPHRITE 1740-1820**—This ovoid shape was designed to be used as a suspended bottle, probably from an ornate stand placed on a table. The grayish white vessel is delicately carved in a stylized leaf tendril design with projecting flanges on the sides, eyelets for the suspension cords, and tassels near the neck. The bottle is hollowed to the utmost thinness. Height: 2 15/16 in. (7.4 cm)
Illustrated: *JICSBS*, March 1981, p. 7, fig. 5.

■ **16. JADEITE 1800-1900**—The artist carved this simple vase shape without decoration to reveal the soft apple green coloring of the natural material, a perfect example of *feicui*, gem quality jade. Height: 2 1/16 in. (5.1 cm)

■ **17. NEPHRITE 1720-1800**—*Petra dura* (hardstone) decoration has been used on snuff bottles throughout the history of their making. This example has been fabricated of a soft gray white jade in an ovoid shape. The scene is a narrative showing a high official seated at a table playing the zither (*qin*); a stand with an elegant incense burner is to his right. On the reverse side are four children playing with various antiques; one of the children is at a table with a cat resting peacefully at his feet. The materials applied to the jade surface are gold, silver, lacquer, jade, coral, turquoise, soapstone, and ivory. The artist has used these materials to create a lively and realistic inner court scene. It is appropriate to mention here that some scholars have attributed this style of work to Japan. Such work was being done in Japan in the late nineteenth and twentieth centuries but there is documentary evidence to confirm the style of work seen here with seventeenth and eighteenth century Chinese craftsmanship. The director of the Museum of Far Eastern Antiquities in Stockholm has written of similar work dating to the Kangxi emperor (see *Arts of Asia*, Nov.-Dec. 1981, p. 112) and like pieces have been documented from the Palace Museum in Taiwan. Decoration of this type is also found on furniture, screens, and boxes of the late Ming and Qing dynasties. Height: 2 1/8 in. (5.3 cm)
See reverse illustration on page 75.
Illustrated: *Arts of Asia*, op. cit., p. 36.

■ **18. JADEITE 1770-1870**—'Floating bottles' refer to minerals carved to utmost thinness enabling the vessel to float in water. This example of the carver's art makes use of an elegant material to reveal the natural transparent coloring of soft blue gray with splashes of green and purple. Height: 2 3/16 in. (5.4 cm)

■ **19. NEPHRITE 1780-1880**—This is another example of a fine old jade bottle of soft amber to russet coloring decorated in hardstone (*petra dura*). Here soapstone has been tinted and partially gilded and lacquered to form the stems of lotus blossoms shielding a duck below and a bird flying overhead. Similar subject matter in an equally interesting design can be seen on the reverse side. Height: 2 3/8 in. (5.5 cm)
Formerly in the collection of Lilla S. Perry.

Description

■ **20. ROCK CRYSTAL 1800-1900**—A clear and colorless crystal bottle is the purest form of quartz. This circular example with a round neck is carved in relief; the design is of a Spanish coin of eight reales. The coin was minted during the reign of Charles III of Spain (1759-1788) for the Mexican Territories. There is a humorous aspect to this creation: the Chinese artisan, not understanding Portuguese, carved the design in reverse. Along with the calligraphy on each face, we see a profile view of the king, and on the opposite side his family coat of arms. Height: 1 3/4 in. (4.8 cm)

■ **21. CRYSTAL 1700-1850**—Early bottles are generally marked by simplicity in shape, ornamentation, and color. This particular vessel is of rectangular form with sloping shoulders tapering toward the base, a finely raised foot, and a well-hollowed interior demonstrating the artisan's fine craftsmanship. Devoid of decoration, the bottle's distinction is derived from its purity of texture and absence of color. Height: 2 3/8 in. (6.0 cm)

■ **22. HAIR CRYSTAL 1750-1850**—An unusual pear-shaped example of the crystalline quartz family contains fiberlike inclusions with impurities of other minerals. In this instance, titanium dioxide is the impurity that produces the reddish brown needles, which add an iridescent sparkle over the surface. Height: 2 1/8 in. (5.3 cm)
Illustrated: *Newsletter*, December 1972, p. 14, fig. 4.

■ **23. HAIR CRYSTAL 1730-1800**—Few hair crystal bottles are as clear and transparent as this example. The inclusions, in this instance tourmaline needles, seem to dart up from the base just as they gushed forth into the crystalline context ages ago. This rectangular form has rounded shoulders and tapers toward the base, while the fine hollowing is the primary reason for the beauty of the crystalline structure. The effect of this bottle reminds one of a monochrome Chinese album leaf. Height: 2 1/4 in. (5.7 cm)
Formerly in the collection of Dwight C. Harris.

■ **24. CRYSTAL 1780-1850**—A purse-shaped vessel such as this was probably made as a presentation piece for a person of rank. The subtle carving on each face illustrates a pair of archaic *chilong* dragons flanking a *shou* (longevity) medallion. It is obvious that the artisan was copying a true fabric purse, because the neck is gathered in folds as if the purse strings were tightened. The carver has placed holes through each side of the top, enabling the vessel to be suspended from around the belt or from a decorative stand. Height: 1 3/4 in. (4.4 cm)

■ **25. HAIR CRYSTAL 1730-1850**—An example of hair crystal similar to no. 23 but with tourmaline needles presenting the effect of autumn grass over the entire surface. The reverse side is more delicately figured, so that the two surfaces give dramatic contrast to each other on this ovoid shaped bottle. Height: 2 3/8 in. (5.9 cm)

■ **26. CRYSTAL 1725-1800**—Smoky crystal is not an uncommon material for snuff bottles, but this unusual one has ten sides, each of which is multi-faceted. A rounded neck projects straight up from one angle and helps dramatize the diamond-like cut of the bottle which in this instance is thinly hollowed. Each face delineates a multi-faceted flower with a concave center. The artist designed this vessel to reveal gradations of tone from light to dark. Height: 2 1/8 in. (5.3 cm)

■ **27. HAIR CRYSTAL 1750-1825**—In this example, the artist has utilized the black tourmaline needles within the transparent crystalline texture to dramatize a high relief carving of a gnarled pine tree. On the upper left corner, an amber colored inclusion was conceived in the form of a hawk descending on one of the branches. The opposite side of the bottle shows no indication of hair-like fibers and is subtly incised, again illustrating a pine tree with birds in flight in the distance. Height: 2 5/8 in. (6.5 cm)

■ **28. CRYSTAL 1736-1795**—This vessel of dark smoky quartz conveying a blackish brown tonality was carved detailing incised inscriptions on both front and reverse sides. The calligraphy is in ancient script but the poems are historically known to be by the Qianlong emperor. The artist has designed the placement of the characters to perfectly fit an eight line stanza divided between the two sides. The bottle is signed *Qianlong yuti*, meaning 'composed by Qianlong.' Height: 2 1/2 in. (6.4 cm)
Formerly in the collection of Martin Schoen.
Illustrated: *Newsletter*, June 1973, p. 5, fig. 3.

Description

■ **29. QUARTZ 1750-1850**—Among the most fanciful bottles are those created by craftsmen using banded agate to reveal lovely abstract patterns that simulate a skyline or a desolate landscape. In this instance, the coloring of the translucent clear material, beautifully hollowed, is made more dramatic by white lines interspersed with dark brown configurations, adding mystery to the scene. Height: 2 1/8 in. (5.3 cm)

■ **30. QUARTZ 1800-1900**—This honey colored, translucent agate is carved in the form of the Chinese citron fruit called a Buddha's hand, *foshou*. The foliage around the neck is hollowed out in areas and the long fingers of the plant are reticulated near the base. The reverse side shows a small butterfly seeking refuge among the fingers of the fruit. Height: 1 15/16 in. (4.9 cm)

■ **31. QUARTZ 1720-1820**—Highly figured agates have been a fascination of Chinese craftsmen for centuries. This example, which is commonly called 'fortification agate,' derives its name solely from the enclosure-like formation nature brought to the material. The vessel is completely undecorated except for the beauty of form and color, which ranges from gray to mauve to rose to white. Height: 2 1/8 in. (5.3 cm)
Illustrated: *JICSBS*, March 1976, p. 6.

■ **32. QUARTZ 1700-1800**—Bloodstone is another of the figured materials that have been sought for making delicate objects over the centuries. This vessel of remarkable coloring ranging from dark green to blood red is undecorated except for carving on the shoulders of the *taotie* masks with rings in their mouths. The perfection of the form, the character of the neck, and the high degree of hollowing on the inside all indicate an early date for this bottle. Height: 2 3/16 in. (5.6 cm)
Formerly in the collection of Martin Schoen.
Exhibited: China Institute. Catalogue, no. 66.
Illustrated: *Newsletter*, December 1972, p. 18, fig. 12.

■ **33. QUARTZ 1800-1900**—This carnelian example of ovoid shape is distinguished by its brilliant color of rust red and a startling white inclusion that resembles a mountain. The reverse side has a smaller flame-like white inclusion. Height: 2 in. (5.1 cm)
Illustrated: *Newsletter*, December 1972, p. 17, fig. 10.

■ **34. PUDDINGSTONE 1750-1825**—The material used for this bottle is a conglomerate of diverse kinds and sizes of stones held together in a sedimentary matrix. Puddingstone pebble inclusions are most frequently of flint, jasper, and other kinds of quartz. This particular example of oval shape with round neck is well hollowed and possesses a concave top with a wide opening. Height: 2 1/4 in. (5.8 cm)
Illustrated: *Newsletter*, December 1972, p. 18, fig. 13.
Illustrated: *Arts of Asia, op. cit.*, col. pl., p. 34.

■ **35. LAPIS LAZULI 1740-1800**—This fine example of rounded rectangular form is completely undecorated except for the *taotie* masks with mock ring handles coming from their mouths. The material appears to be like other stones which come from the rich lapis deposits in Russia. China imported these rocks for many centuries to decorate ornamental pieces and it is likely that this classic form was fashioned in the eighteenth century. Height: 2 5/16 in. (5.7 cm)
Formerly in the collection of Martin Schoen.

■ **36. FOSSILIFEROUS LIMESTONE 1800-1870**—Limestone is composed primarily of calcite. In this instance, varying forms and shapes of fossils, more than likely of marine origin, can be seen to form a fascinating abstract design in subtle colors of gray, rose, and off-white. It was more than obvious to the creator of this vessel that further decoration was not necessary. Height: 2 1/2 in. (6.4 cm)
Formerly in the collection of Lilla S. Perry.
Illustrated: Perry, *op. cit.*, p. 64, no. 44.

■ **37. LAPIS LAZULI 1800-1880**—Flattened ovoid shapes such as the sample seen here were often designed to be placed in a sleeve or the girdle of a garment. In this undecorated example, the beauty of the natural material is its most persuasive characteristic. The brilliant use of blue mixed with a dominant matrix produces an unusual abstract design. The material is similar to other examples observed in Buddhist sculptures, and probably originates in Afghanistan. Height: 2 7/16 in. (6.0 cm)
Formerly in the collection of Martin Schoen.
Illustrated: *JICSBS*, March 1976, p. 7.

Description

■**38. SOAPSTONE 1740-1800**—Steatite is another name for this material which is the softest of stones. It is characterized by an oily texture and the colors range from buff to russet as in this example. The spade shape with flaring neck and original matching stopper is the finest of its type known to this author. The scene illustrates a convocation of the eighteen Luohans—a theme used by Chinese artisans for centuries and especially in the Qing dynasty. Each Luohan has a distinct physiognomy and is holding his particular attribute. One side shows a rampant dragon, which appears to be supporting the figures in their celestial abode. The intaglio ground area is carved in a subtle cloud motif, and at the lowest level we see a wave pattern. The base and neck are in the key-fret motif, with the stylized leaf pattern terminating the neck. While unsigned, this example has all the attributes of the imperial workshops and follows the style of the early dated ivory bottles of the Qianlong period. Height: 2 13/16 in. (7.1 cm)
See reverse illustration on page 75.
Formerly in the collection of Martin Schoen.
Exhibited: China Institute. Catalogue, no. 72.
Illustrated: *Arts of Asia, op. cit.*, col. pl., p. 35.

■**39. JASPER 1780-1850**—The vessel is an unusual example: two colors help define a high relief carving illustrating a monkey seated under a pine tree. He contemplates a deer on the upper right and a bird and moth below. The material is another example of the cryptocrystalline category of quartz, and the reverse side illustrates the opaque but lustrous texture of the natural stone. Height: 2 1/2 in. (6.4 cm)
Formerly in the collection of Lilla S. Perry.
Illustrated: Perry, *op. cit.*, p. 62, no. 40.
Illustrated: *Newsletter*, December 1972, p. 18, fig. 11.

■**40. CALCITE 1700-1800**—The monkey king is said to have gone to heaven and stolen some peaches from the tree belonging to the Queen Mother of the West, Xiwangmu. The monkey, carrying a large branch of peaches, is here enshrined in cloud formations. The reverse shows a delightful tan and brown abstract design natural to travertine marble. Height: 2 5/8 in. (6.6 cm)

■**41. CHALCEDONY 1750-1860**—One of the most popular subjects to the agate carver is the one seen here. The high relief carving of the horse tethered to a finely detailed post with brick base is dramatically silhouetted against a translucent natural ground. Hovering above is the ever-present winged bat and to the side and behind the horse is an inquisitive monkey seated on a rock. The reverse side is completely plain, helping to focus interest in the prime subjects. Height: 2 3/4 in. (7.0 cm)
Formerly in the collections of Georgia Roode and Ralph M. Hults.

■**42. CHALCEDONY 1780-1850**—Large and translucent colored agates with opaque areas are ideal mediums for cameo-style carving. This example details a Chinese unicorn, *qilin*, at the bottom, a pine branch with an eagle above, and a bat on a cloud to the far right. The reverse side details mandarin ducks in a lotus pond, all of which are opaque in tone against the translucent honey colored ground. Height: 2 13/16 in. (7.2 cm)

■**43. CHALCEDONY 1760-1850**—This bottle of unusual and subtle coloring belongs to the agate family. The design is in high relief and illustrates a ram resting under a gnarled pine tree with a bat on the upper right and the magical *lingzhi* or fungus by the pine trunk. The ground area is of a deep gray brown tonality adding subtle contrast to the scene. The reverse side is deftly carved showing a duck wading in a lotus pond with incised carving of waves in contrast to the relief carving of the lotus pond. Height: 2 9/16 in. (6.8 cm)
Formerly in the collections of Georgia Roode and Ralph M. Hults.

38

39

40

41

42

43

Description

■ **44. CHALCEDONY 1750-1850**—Shadow agates are among the most fascinating snuff bottle textures. This ovoid example is carved to emphasize the cameo, or relief-style, carving at its best. One face illustrates the bearded Shoulao, God of Longevity, with a bat near his feet. The figure approaches an open pavilion on the precipice of a mountain with pine branches and a crescent moon overhead. On the opposite side, the central dark inclusion shows a ram by a rocky ledge; a crane is in the lighter natural ground to the side. The symbols mean good fortune and immortality. Height: 2 3/8 in. (6.0 cm)

■ **45. CHALCEDONY 1700-1780**—The Suzhou school is again represented by a unique example. This ovoid shape with elongated neck and rim foot is carved in varying degrees of relief dramatically detailing the design in blackish brown tones on a clear to honey colored ground. The principal face shows a sage in a rocky grotto to whom a book is brought by an attendant. To the right are additional rock formations and a large pine branch hovering over the heads of the figures. The reverse side is clear except for one dark spot carved in the form of a bird perched on a rock, again part of a grotto. To the left are three lines of calligraphy finely carved in relief; they can be translated as follows: 'Having mastered the secret of immortality, one would no longer count the comings and goings of spring.' Height: 2 3/16 in. (5.6 cm)
See reverse illustration on page 75.
Illustrated: *Arts of Asia, op. cit.*, p. 37.

■ **46. CHALCEDONY 1750-1850**—Another example of a shadow agate of transparent texture is seen here including dark inclusions which serve to highlight the *petra dura* decoration on each face. It is possible that the decoration was done at a later date than the actual fabrication of the bottle itself. In the scene, a sage is being attended by a young boy; nearby are household utensils and a table with a spray of flowers. The reverse side appears to be related to this domestic scene. A lady prepares food on a large Ming-style table, while a little boy carries vessels on a tray to his master. Height: 2 3/8 in. (6.0 cm)

■ **47. CHALCEDONY 1740-1825**—This shadow agate humorously depicts the playful Liu Hai with his string of cash standing on his closest ally, the three-legged toad, in turn supported by a floating lotus leaf. The use of a bluish gray tone for the central figures is impressive against a honey colored agate ground. The reverse side is subtly carved illustrating lotuses emanating from a water pond. Height: 2 9/16 in. (6.8 cm)
Illustrated: *JICSBS*, June 1973, p. 7, fig. 9.

■ **48. CHALCEDONY 1800-1875**—This bottle of ovoid shape with a long round neck is a fine example of the cryptocrystalline form of chalcedony. The almost opaque brown tone of the material is carved in high relief depicting a delightful and whimsical scene. A monkey perched on a rock supports himself partially from a pine tree branch, but one foot is on the back of a pony whose leash he holds in his right hand. Each looks at the other, wondering what will happen next. The scene is a rebus which can be read: 'May you soon be elevated to the rank of Marquis.' The reverse side of the bottle is plain except for the continuation of the pine branch and a pair of cranes with a butterfly on the side. Height: 2 3/16 in. (5.6 cm)

■ **49. CHALCEDONY 1820-1900**—A natural quartz texture with a green skin has been carved to include a chloretic inclusion in the bottle. The artist has confined the inclusion to one specific area and carved a large but youthful looking Buddhist lion playing with the familiar brocaded and beribboned ball. The reverse side is completely plain. Height: 2 7/16 in. (6.1 cm)

■ **50. CHALCEDONY 1750-1825**—True cameo-style carving is illustrated in this agate bottle which, on the reverse side, is plain except for the material's color variations. The main face, however, is dramatically carved bringing out the three tonalities within the material. The outermost layer shows a horse tethered to a tree on a rocky terrain. The next level shows a willow tree in a dark brown tonality and the third level is the natural warm gray ground. Height: 2 3/16 in. (5.6 cm)

44

45

46

47

48

49

50

Description

■ **51. TOURMALINE 1780-1880**—This triangular bottle of rich deep rose tourmaline belongs to the complex mineral cyclosilicate. This example reveals richness of color by reserving the carving for the sides and showing a simple leaf motif on each face. The side panels are detailed with a pair of squirrels climbing a fruit tree vine. As we know, tourmaline was used in China throughout the snuff bottle period, therefore vessels such as this could well have been made in the eighteenth century, though the great majority of tourmaline bottles were produced in the nineteenth and twentieth centuries when imports were made from Brazil and America, as well as Sri Lanka. Height: 1 15/16 in. (5.0 cm)

■ **52. TURQUOISE 1750-1850**—This superlative old turquoise, carved in a spade shape, is a rare example. The variation in color seen on both faces is due to porosity of the material, which makes it permeable to chemicals so that age and handling naturally change the color of the basic material. One side shows an ancient ceremonial bronze in relief, while the opposite side shows a medallion with four lines of archaic script which reads: 'Xi Ji Fu made this precious *dui* vessel for Zhong Qiang to be used and treasured forever from generation to generation.' The wide neck, the deep hollowing, the color, and the brown matrix help assign this bottle to an early date. Height: 2 3/16 in. (5.6 cm)
Formerly in the collection of Dwight C. Harris.
Illustrated: Stevens, *op. cit.*, nos. 608, 623.
Illustrated: *JICSBS*, September 1977, p. 12, fig. 8.
Illustrated: *Arts of Asia, op. cit.*, p. 33.

■ **53. TOURMALINE 1850-1900**—The rare color combination seen on this bottle implies that the material was imported into China and made by a master carver. The jet black ground area is fashioned into a fruit resembling a peach. The surrounding area is a rich rose tonality, the most popular tourmaline color, and carved almost free from the black core on the sides and on one face. This area details a high relief carving of He Xiangu holding a fly whisk and her ever-present flower basket. To one side is a young attendant and to the other side is a gnarled branch with a crane.
Height: 1 15/16 in. (5.0 cm)
Formerly in the collections of Dwight C. Harris and Martin Schoen.
Exhibited: Hong Kong Museum of Art, October 20-December 3, 1978. Catalogue of an exhibition, *Snuff Bottles of the Ch'ing Dynasty*, col. pl., no. 247. Subsequently referred to as: Catalogue.
Illustrated: *Newsletter*, December 1972, p. 19, fig. 18.

■ **54. AQUAMARINE 1750-1850**—This material, which belongs to the beryl family, was available in the entire snuff bottle period but early examples are rare. The material is known to have been imported from Siberia during the eighteenth century and the example illustrated is of such clarity and simplicity, as well as a high degree of hollowing, that one is inclined to attribute this bottle to the early period. Carved in flattened vase form, the vessel is without decoration except for the translucence of the soft blue green color. Height: 2 5/8 in. (6.6 cm)
Formerly in the collection of Lilla S. Perry.

■ **55. AMETHYST 1850-1900**—Crystalline quartz is the mineral from which this material emanates and its beautiful purple color is caused by small amounts of manganese within the stone. The deep gem-like tonality of this example is carved with *chilong* dragons ascending one side and a spray of the Chinese magic fungus, *lingzhi*, descending on the opposite side. The original stopper is appropriately surmounted with another *chilong*. It is interesting to note that the dragon on the right side is in a clear crystal tonality implying that the impurities did not reach this area. Height: 1 15/16 in. (5.0 cm)
Formerly in the collection of Martin Schoen.
Illustrated: *Newsletter*, December 1972, p. 15, fig. 6.
Illustrated: *JICSBS*, March 1981, p. 10, fig. 15.

■ **56. AQUAMARINE 1750-1825**—This subject has been depicted on every type of snuff bottle and always is represented as the happy boy, Liu Hai, holding a string of cash with the three-legged toad at his feet. This miniature carving in aquamarine was detailed with great finesse by a master carver. Another toad in rose quartz serves as a stopper on the head of the figure. Tradition tells us that the mythical three-legged toad was considered to be an animated purse full of coins and thereby a symbol of wealth. Height: 2 in. (5.1 cm)
Illustrated: *Newsletter*, December 1972, p. 20, fig. 19.
Illustrated: *Newsletter*, June 1978, p. 7, fig. 10.

■ **57. MALACHITE 1860-1940**—Malachite was known to have been available to Chinese craftsmen throughout the snuff bottle period. It was probably imported from the Ural Mountain area of Russia. It is also known to have been used on dated seventeenth and eighteenth century pieces and studded bronze sculptures in Tibet and Mongolia. The ovoid shape of this small vessel is beautifully grained and carved, with the traditional cat and butterfly theme in a rocky garden landscape on one side and what appears to be a rat in a garden on the opposite side. Height: 1 13/16 in. (4.6 cm)

■ **58. SAPPHIRE 1850-1925**—The corundum mineral family is an uncommon material throughout the snuff bottle period. This circular vessel is without decoration except for the deep blue coloring with highlights common to sapphire stones. While the material is not frequently seen except in modern snuff bottles, this example shows signs of handling, has a wide mouth and is very well hollowed, indicating a somewhat earlier date. Height: 1 7/8 in. (4.7 cm)

■ **59. EMBELLISHED MALACHITE 1800-1900**—Tour de force is the term that best describes this masterpiece of design and craftsmanship. The rectangular shape, tapering toward the base, is fabricated of a highly figured malachite overlaid with lacquer forming brown branches and soapstone detailing magnolia blossoms and the wings of the butterflies on each side. The bodies of the butterflies are made of coral and studded with mother-of-pearl and jadeite. Height: 2 3/8 in. (6.0 cm)
Formerly in the collection of Lilla S. Perry.
Illustrated: Perry, *op. cit.*, p. 143, no. 149.
Illustrated: *Arts of Asia, op. cit.*, p. 37.

51 52 53

54 55 56

57 58 59

Description

■ **60. CORAL 1770-1870**—The soft, even tones of this coral bottle are heightened by the high relief carving of a rampant buffalo being tamed by a young groom with clouds above. The reverse side illustrates a lady riding on a horse, attended by her servant with a banner, outside the city walls. The name of the lady is Mulan, in the act of preparing for a battle to defend her country. The distinctiveness of the stopper on this bottle, though not original, bears special mention as it is a gem quality imperial jade with a white jade collar. Height: 2 7/16 in. (6.1 cm)
Illustrated: *JICSBS*, March 1976, p. 7.
Illustrated: *Arts of Asia, op. cit.*, p. 37.

■ **61. IVORY 1780-1880**—Fine ivory carving is an old craft in China. Pieces were cut from the solid areas of elephant and walrus tooth and then carved in studios set apart for this specialty. This ovoid example illustrates an elderly sage seated on a rock under a willow tree. His attendant appears to hold a hoe, which he may be using to cut a fungus plant emanating from a large rock formation. The reverse shows a fisherman seated at the water's edge with an attendant taking in the catch. The neck has the key-fret motif leading into a stylized leaf pattern on both the neck and original matching stopper. Height: 2 1/8 in. (5.3 cm)
Illustrated: *Newsletter*, September 1971, front cover.

■ **62. CORAL 1880-1930**—Cabinet bottles were a late development in the fabrication of snuff bottles. The form seen here is an excellent example of the carver's virtuosity, but hardly a functional vessel for snuff. Nevertheless, collectors have sought them primarily for the beauty of the material as well as the dexterity displayed by the artisan. One face of the bottle shows a boy standing on a rock, holding a flowering lotus branch on which a bird perches. Below, we see a large cat ready to climb a rock to catch the bird, which is naively peering down at a basket of fruit suspended from the branch of a tree. The reverse side illustrates an elegant goddess, in flowing robes, holding a peony blossom branch. An original matching stopper completes this rich display piece. Height: 2 7/16 in. (6.1 cm)
Illustrated: *Arts of Asia, op. cit.*, p. 36.

■ **63. IVORY 1800-1880**—This is a documentary bottle, for the artist has signed his name, Runsheng. Along with the inscription and a studio seal, a beautiful poem is carved in raised calligraphy. The translation is: 'Suddenly I see the winter prunus trees blossoming by the Han River. Not realizing that spring comes so early, I take the little flowers to be pearls.' The opposite side visually illustrates the text by showing lovely prunus blossoms emanating from a gnarled branch over a rocky ground. A pair of archaic *chilong* dragons envelop the shoulders and neck of the bottle with their foliated tails flanking its sides. Height: 2 3/4 in. (7.0 cm)
Formerly in the collection of H. J. Heinz.

■ **64. TRIPLE OVERLAY LACQUER ON METAL 1736-1795**—Bottles made by imperial command were for the delectation of the Emperor and his court. This example is of a triple overlay of cinnabar red on dark green, on top of a yellow ochre ground, with each layer carved to give depth and beauty to the overall composition. One face illustrates an imperial lady at a table in the act of writing, with three attendants. The reverse side illustrates a high official, attended by four persons, listening to musicians playing the flute on the terrace of a pavilion. The dark green foliage is luxuriously rendered and the ochre ground forms the backdrop. The base has a finely incised inscription, *Qianlong nianzhi* (made in the Qianlong period). Beijing palace workshops. Height: 3 1/8 in. (8.0 cm)
Formerly in the collection of Martin Schoen.
Exhibited: China Institute. Catalogue, no. 71.
Illustrated: *JICSBS*, December 1974, front cover.
Illustrated: *Arts of Asia, op. cit.*, col. pl., p. 35.

■ **65. MAMMOTH TOOTH 1600-1700**—The fossilized mammoth tooth is one of the rare materials imported into China, possibly before the use of snuff. Bob C. Stevens has suggested that vessels of this type may have originally been used as medicine bottles in the fifteenth and sixteenth centuries, since the bottle in his collection and this one bear a striking similarity and show distinct signs of handling as well as wide necks and extensive hollowing uncommon to this material. The circular form with long neck is without decoration except for the beautiful abstract designs inherent in the material. Height: 2 9/16 in. (6.5 cm)

■ **66. CINNABAR LACQUER 1800-1880**—The flattened baluster form is an unusual shape for a cinnabar lacquer bottle. The carving is executed with maximum dexterity and illustrates two boys playing with a fanciful Buddhist lion. The reverse shows a young boy in a verdant landscape with flowering peonies. The artist has achieved a high degree of animation in this delicate scene. The base has an incised four-character seal of the Qianlong emperor but it is probably not of the period. Height: 3 1/16 in. (7.8 cm)

60
61
62
63
64
65
66

Description

■ **67. EMBELLISHED AMBER 1720-1800**—Old amber bottles were frequently carved with *taotie* masks and mock ring handles on the sides. However, embellished amber bottles are relatively rare. Jade, agate, amber, ivory, soapstone, and lacquer are here used in a consummate manner to illustrate a court scene of a lady with attendants presenting gifts in a garden setting. The narrative continues on the reverse side and illustrates a high official about to receive gifts from his subordinates. The style and period of this bottle are similar to that of the jade bottle, no. 17. Height: 2 3/16 in. (5.5 cm)
Formerly in the collection of Lilla S. Perry.
Illustrated: *Arts of Asia, op. cit.*, col. pl., p. 35.

■ **68. AMBER 1780-1850**—This elongated vessel, which is very well hollowed, is a supreme example of this carver's art. The entire surface is carved to illustrate an ascending dragon in high relief seeking the elusive pearl. In this instance, an actual pearl is inset on each face. The pearl, on the reverse side, is caught by the five claws of the dragon. The eyes of the dragon are inlaid with yellow mother-of-pearl and the pupils are set in jet. Swirling clouds surround the dragon in his quest for the prized pearls. An original matching stopper completes this magnificent composition. On the base are two Chinese characters, *Danshan*. A literal translation means 'cinnabar mountain;' this must be an assumed name of the maker, however, since the signature appears on three known bottles by the same hand. Height: 3 11/16 in. (9.4 cm)
Formerly in the collection of Martin Schoen.
Exhibited: China Institute. Catalogue, no. 76.
Illustrated: Stevens, *op. cit.*, nos. 718, 719.
Illustrated: *Arts of Asia, op. cit.*, col. pl., p. 31.

■ **69. AMBER 1780-1880**—The material seen in this example is known as root amber and varies in tone from ochre on the face to dark brown on the reverse. The natural form is carved in high relief with a famous sage on a donkey followed by his attendant holding a spray of prunus blossoms, known as 'searching for plum blossoms in the snow.' Arching over the entire composition is a large grotto shaped by blossoming prunus trees. Height: 2 5/16 in. (5.7 cm)
Exhibited: Hong Kong Museum of Art. Catalogue, col. pl., no. 249.
Illustrated: *JICSBS*, June 1975, p. 22.
Illustrated: *Arts of Asia, op. cit.*, col. pl., p. 34.

■ **70. MOTHER-OF-PEARL 1650-1750**—Early snuff bottles of this material are rare, but this example demonstrates all of the functional and aesthetic attributes of a seventeenth or eighteenth century vessel. The mellow texture is carved to follow the natural form of the material, showing much handling as indicated by the concave detail on one face. The carving resembles an archaic dragon but it is so subtle that the identification cannot be definite. The right side shows a vase with a *lingzhi*, Chinese fungus, emanating from it. Rings project from the upper part of the neck. An incised inscription on the base reads: *Gusongxuan* or 'Ancient Pine Studio.' Height: 2 5/16 in. (5.9 cm)
Illustrated: *JICSBS*, March 1976, p. 7.

■ **71. WALRUS IVORY 1750-1850**—This vessel of rounded rectangular form with a long circular neck has been dyed to simulate malachite or maybe an emerald green jade. Most examples of the walrus type are plain, but this one has been minutely carved to show a Chinese unicorn, *qilin*, and a rabbit amid bamboo and pine trees. The reverse shows the famous scene of the monkey feeding peaches to the deer. *Taotie* masks with mock ring handles are on the sides. Height: 2 3/8 in. (6.0 cm)

■ **72. JET 1800-1900**—Petrified coal is the material used to create this flattened vase with a smooth satin finish. The face is finely incised in a medallion form with archaic script translated as follows: 'Mengjian made this *ding* [bronze vessel] to be treasured from generation to generation.' In the center is the name of the artist, Shixiang. The reverse is incised in dull gold illustrating willow trees, rocks, and houses. Height: 1 15/16 in. (4.9 cm)

■ **73. LAQUE BURGAUTÉ ON METAL 1780-1880**—The Chinese originated the technique of incising and inlaying mother-of-pearl on a lacquer ground as early as the Tang dynasty. This oblong ovoid shape is lacquered on all surfaces in a brownish black tonality and inlaid with iridescent shells tinted in different pastel colors. Full peony blossoms and foliage can be seen with two birds on the upper left. Gold and shell particles form a diaper pattern on the flat side panels curving around the neck. The design is repeated on the original matching stopper. The base of this bottle is unmarked. Height: 2 13/16 in. (7.1 cm)

■ **74. COCONUT SHELL Dated 1872**—Two sections of shell have been joined together to form this medallion shape. The front of the bottle has a long prose passage which has been translated: 'It is better to be a farmer enjoying nature rather than a politician letting the people suffer bad times.' Another inscription follows: 'In the eighth month of the *renshen* year of the Tongzhi period, I carved this for Weijian,' signed 'Lanpo of Wumen (Jiangsu Province).' The reverse is incised to show two rugged beasts with a descriptive poem on the upper left side giving the date as mid-autumn of the *renshen* year and the signature of Zhu Xiqing. Height: 2 1/8 in. (5.3 cm)
Exhibited: Hong Kong Museum of Art. Catalogue, no. 150.

67
68
69
70
71
72
73
74

Description

■ **75. HORNBILL IVORY 1750-1850**—The hermited hornbill or *rhinoplax vigil* is a bird native to the Malay Archipelago. The bottle seen here is of a rectangular shape with rounded shoulders and base. The caramel colored material is polished to a rich luster and the only decoration is on the sides, which forms the red sheath common to this bird. In this instance, the sheath is carved to illustrate two monkeys snatching fruit from tree branches on each side. The simplicity of the design and its delicate execution lead one to an eighteenth century date, knowing that Chinese nobility was fascinated by rare materials. Documentary bottles are known to exist in the imperial collections in the National Palace Museum in Taiwan, including hornbill ivory fashioned into archers' rings, buckles, and hair ornaments.
Illustrated: *JICSBS*, March 1976, p. 7.

■ **76. HORNBILL IVORY Dated 1843**—This delicate, spade-shaped design is subtly carved on one face illustrating a Chinese unicorn, *qilin*, reaching toward the sun. The soft red sheath on the sides is carved in the traditional *taotie* masks with double mock ring handles. The opposite side has finely incised calligraphy in archaic and standard scripts, followed by two seals of the artist, *Baishi*. The inscription ends with the words: 'Master Jiade made this bottle for his own use.' Height: 2 1/16 in. (5.1 cm)
See reverse illustration on page 75.
Illustrated: *Arts of Asia, op. cit.*, p. 36.

■ **77. AMBER 1750-1825**—Baltic amber is one of the highly sought after materials in China because of its beautiful yellow coloring. This rectangular example with sloping shoulders is particularly lush in color, and a natural fault in the material has been deftly carved by the artist in the form of a *lingzhi* fungus branch on which a bird lingers. The opposite side illustrates a lotus branch with large foliage and a kingfisher bird. Height: 2 5/8 in. (6.6 cm)

■ **78. EMBELLISHED WOOD 1800-1900**—An unusual horseshoe-shaped bottle made of purple sandalwood, *zitan*, is embellished with large panels of mother-of-pearl on each face. One side shows a traditional pavilion with a scholar seated at a table within a rocky garden. The opposite side is similar but includes a mountain scene and pavilion with two scholars. The darker sky tonality gives distinct contrast to the opposite face. The sides of the bottle are inlaid with a fret pattern of *laque burgauté* adding another distinctive feature to an atypical bottle. Height: 3 in. (7.6 cm)
Formerly in the collections of Lilla S. Perry and Ralph M. Hults.
Illustrated: Perry, *op. cit.*, p. 119, no. 119.

■ **79. EMBELLISHED LACQUER ON METAL 1736-1795**—The only scholar to research embellished bottles has been Bob C. Stevens in *The Collector's Book of Snuff Bottles*, pages 222 through 226. This author concurs with his judgment that bottles of the type seen here are completely of Chinese craftsmanship. The references cited for an embellished nephrite bottle, no. 17, also apply to the materials and techniques used here. We see a royal lady reclining on a *kang* (day bed) while holding a golden *ruyi* scepter. A dwarf servant carries a box to her. Adjacent to her bed is a large screen and a garden stool. The entire scene is beside a fantastic large rock formation. The reverse side reveals two other colorfully costumed dwarfs holding musical instruments with tree branches flanking a dancing crane. This vignette is next to huge rocks and a flowering plum tree which envelops the entire upper part of the bottle. The imperial reign mark, *Qianlong nianzhi* (made in the Qianlong period) is precisely inscribed on the base in formal seal script. Height: 3 3/8 in. (8.6 cm)

■ **80. IVORY 1750-1825**—Elephants were almost extinct in China proper, requiring their importation from India and even Africa as early as the Ming dynasty. Nevertheless, ivory was considered an important material in the minds of the artisans. This double gourd shape is profusely carved in the round with a continuous design of intertwining leaves, flowers, and insects including butterflies and grasshoppers. Miniature gourds also enhance the surface, which culminates in a perfectly matched stopper as part of the total design. Height: 3 3/8 in. (8.5 cm)
Illustrated: *JICSBS*, June 1976, p. 14, fig. 1.

■ **81. TORTOISESHELL 1850-1925**—An unusual material has been formed into an attractive shape by the joining of two sections with a seam in the center. The neck and base have been added, and a matching stopper completes the vessel to give a completely autonomous appearance. The material is transparent which adds much to its beauty when seen with light passing through. The bottle may or may not have been a functional vessel but its engrossing shape and beautiful material make it a unique addition to the collection. Height: 2 5/16 in. (5.9 cm)

75

76

77

78

79

80

81

Description

■ **82. BRONZE Dated 1652**—This vessel is one of the earliest documented snuff bottles showing the reign mark of the emperor, Shunzhi. Of rounded rectangular form, it is chased in bold lines showing two dragons seeking the flaming pearl on each face. Stylized clouds that echo the *ruyi* scepter shape add richness to the surface. After the casting, the craftsman rendered the dragon's body and the flames issuing from the pearls in a technique achieved with a punching instrument. Each of the shoulders has a raised panel in which butterflies are incised. An original matching stopper coordinated in design with the bottle completes the composition. The base is inscribed, 'made by Cheng Rongzhang in the ninth year of the Shunzhi period.' Height: 2 7/16 in. (6.2 cm)
Formerly in the collection of Martin Schoen.
Exhibited: China Institute. Catalogue, no. 82.
Exhibited: Hong Kong Museum of Art. Catalogue, no. 1.
Illustrated: *Arts of Asia, op. cit.,* col. pl., p. 34.

■ **83. SILVER 1800-1900**—A true miniature vase has been adapted for snuff with a bold dragon, applied in relief, wrapped swirlingly around the bottle from the neck to the base. The base has a rectangular seal which reads *Juji*, and a small seal with the letters HK—perhaps meaning a studio in Hong Kong. Height: 1 3/4 in. (4.4 cm)
Formerly in the collection of Henry Walters.

■ **84. CLOISONNÉ 1740-1825**—The technique of applying multicolored enamels between thin wires on a metal ground was introduced into China during the Ming dynasty. Here on each side are highly stylized floral motifs surrounded by foliage in primary colors. The design and the colors of this example can be seen on documented eighteenth century pieces, but the style continued to be produced into the nineteenth century. Shields on each shoulder, incised to resemble the *taotie* masks, are in a pewter finish, while the neck and the base are obviously of brass. Height: 2 1/8 in. (5.4 cm)

■ **85. EMBELLISHED METAL 1780-1880**—This silver gilt ovoid vessel is inlaid with enamels and glass. The front and back panels are decorated with formalized floral medallions in green, blue, and lavender on a filigree ground. The side ribs are inlaid with baguettes of red glass, completing this elegant bottle with an original matching stopper. Height: 2 3/8 in. (6.0 cm)

■ **86. COPPER REPOUSSÉ 1800-1900**—Here is an unusual, highly stylized representation of the Eight Daoist Immortals amid the clouds. The figures are in high relief and are replete with their respective attributes. The base has a lappet motif and the neck has a stylized leaf pattern terminating in a flaring neck and an original matching stopper. The *baxian* or Eight Immortals take their origin from Daoist lore derived from centuries of antiquity. While three of them are known to have been historical personages, each is empowered with the ability to perform magic and achieve various transformations. Height: 2 1/2 in. (6.3 cm)

■ **87. EMBELLISHED SILVER 1800-1875**—The entire perimeter of China, including Mongolia and Tibet, came under the influence of the Manzus. It is interesting to note that among the older population, snuff taking is still popular today in the outer regions. This vessel is of distinct Mongolian origin with medallions on each face inset with turquoise, coral, and malachite. The side panels and the original matching stopper are studded in a similar manner. The base flares out at the bottom and the overall design gives an appearance of being extensively used. Height: 2 1/8 in. (5.3 cm)

■ **88. CLOISONNÉ 1800-1880**—This enameled snuff bottle on a copper ground has been elegantly designed to illustrate three butterflies on each face surrounded by flowers and foliage. The ovoid shape with long rounded neck follows a tradition that was repeated many times in the nineteenth century and this example illustrates the style achieved with multicolored values of blue, green, yellow, and russet. Height: 2 3/16 in. (5.6 cm)

■ **89. INCISED WHITE METAL 1775-1850**—*Baitong* is the proper name of the Chinese white metal used for this bottle of rounded rectangular form. The alloy is achieved by the combination of tin and zinc. The vessel is delicately incised to illustrate a cat watching a butterfly on one face and a fanciful demon on the opposite side. Each medallion is surrounded by a pair of prancing dragons forming an ovoid pattern. The long neck has a traditional lappet border and includes an original matching stopper. Height: 2 13/16 in. (7.2 cm)

■ **90. GOLD 1925-1930**—A series of bottles was made by Lee King Yee during the years mentioned here, as confirmed by his grandson. Each bottle was fabricated of 22-carat gold and was cast by the lost wax process. Mr. Lee was born in 1886 in Guangdong Province and apprenticed as a goldsmith with his uncle. He became a master of his craft in China and moved to San Francisco in 1924. It was during this later period that he made a series of bottles illustrating the four seasons. This example is one of three still known to his family. One face illustrates a bird on a prunus blossom branch with rocks below. The reverse shows a traditional mountain landscape with pine trees. This work, with its original matching stopper and base, is equal to the finest craftsmanship of earlier days. Height: 1 15/16 in. (4.9 cm)

82 83 84

85 86 87

88 89 90

Description

■ **91. ENAMELS ON METAL 1736-1795**—
European subject matter was popular in eighteenth century Beijing due to the presence of Jesuit priests, artists, and missionaries. This fine vase shape is enameled on copper with the entire palette of *famille rose* colors. The yellow and blue bands around the top and base add contrast to the subtle colors of the primary subjects. The bottle illustrates a young lady holding a small dog on her shoulder, with a typical Renaissance-style architectural landscape in the background. The reverse side shows another lady in much the same setting. The borders at the top and bottom of the bottle are finely detailed scroll motifs with a traditional wave pattern around the neck. The base is inscribed in blue, *Qianlong nianzhi* (made in the Qianlong period). This bottle came from the Beijing workshops. Height: 1 13/16 in. (4.6 cm)
Illustrated: *Arts of Asia, op. cit.*, col. pl., p. 34.

■ **92. ENAMELS ON METAL 1770-1795**—
Festive garden scenes at court are popular themes for snuff bottles. This flattened vase form with a long neck is polychromed on copper. Seventeen persons are illustrated, all showing a sense of joy in a beautiful landscape scene of trees and rocks. The borders at the neck and the base include the key-fret motif as well as the *ruyi* lappets in an iron red color. The base is inscribed in blue, *jingzhi* (respectfully made) in seal script. This bottle can thus be attributed to the palace workshops in Beijing. Height: 2 1/4 in. (5.8 cm)
Formerly in the collections of Christian Holmes and Martin Schoen.
Exhibited: China Institute. Catalogue, no. 22.
Illustrated: Stevens, *op. cit.*, no. 986.
Illustrated: *Arts of Asia, op. cit.*, p. 35.

■ **93. ENAMELS ON METAL 1736-1795**—
While the technique of enameling did not originate in China, the Chinese produced a vast number of elegant miniature vessels for the fancy of the court and high ranking officials. This ovoid shape with enamels on a copper ground shows elderly sages conversing by a pine tree in a verdant landscape. The opposite side shows two additional sages contemplating in a rocky landscape. The decoration at the neck and the base is unusually simple. The base is inscribed in blue, *Qianlong nianzhi* (made in the Qianlong period). This is a product of the Beijing palace workshops. Height: 1 15/16 in. (5.0 cm)

■ **94. ENAMELS ON METAL 1750-1820**—
Simple ovoid shapes are common to polychromed enamels on a copper ground. The decoration here is uncommon in that it shows a pond with lotuses including large leaves and delicately rendered blossoms. Kingfishers and mandarin ducks complete this scene, which runs continuously around the bottle. The neck and base of this bottle have the key-fret motif with a lappet border just below the neckline. The base has the traditional inscription in black, *Qianlong nianzhi* (made in the Qianlong period). The bottle appears to be of the Beijing palace workshops but may be later than the reign mark given. Height: 1 15/16 in. (5.0 cm)

■ **95. ENAMELS ON METAL 1750-1820**—
This pear-shaped vessel has vibrant polychromed enamels on a copper ground. The scene illustrates a pair of pheasants on a rock in a bamboo landscape. The reverse shows a mountain landscape with a pagoda and houses. Each of these medallions is encased by a fine dull yellow border which is stippled and includes delicately rendered flowers and foliage in multicolors. The neck and lower band details are coordinated with this very stylized design. On the base we see the traditional inscription in blue, *Qianlong nianzhi* (made in the Qianlong period). Again, the bottle may be later than the reign mark indicated. Height: 1 13/16 in. (4.6 cm)

■ **96. ENAMELS ON METAL 1750-1820**—
This elongated form is common to the Guangzhou workshops during the eighteenth and nineteenth centuries. The design of multicolored peonies and other flowers with delicate foliage and running vine motifs covers the entire bottle. Along with the *famille rose* flowers, the cobalt blue ground creates a contrasting floral setting. Height: 2 3/8 in. (6.0 cm)

■ **97. ENAMELS ON METAL 1750-1820**—
Guangzhou work frequently resembles the Beijing school. In this example, one face illustrates two boys playing with a dog in a garden setting. The reverse shows a man and his lady in a typical Western architectural garden setting. The area surrounding the scenes is stippled in yellow with peonies finely drawn in multicolors. Instead of a traditional reign mark, the base has a repeat of one of the floral patterns with a yellow ground from the surround of the bottle. This feature is common to the Guangzhou workshops. Height: 2 1/16 in. (5.2 cm)

■ **98. ENAMELS ON COPPER 1780-1880**—
The majority of Guangzhou polychromed enamels have design characteristics making them recognizable as products of the southern seaport, as in the vase-shaped example. The design on this vessel is highly stylized and shows a ragged peony, *baoxianghua*, or precious image flower, in pink, and above, a bat of the same color on each side. The balance of the bottle is rendered in foliage and small blossoms in aqua tones, all on a yellow ground. Height: 2 5/16 in. (5.9 cm)

91

92

93

94

95

96

97

98

Description

■ **99. ENAMELS ON GLASS 1736-1795—**
Polychromed enamel decoration on glass was among the most active crafts in the Beijing palace compound. This example illustrates sophisticated techniques in design and painting. One face shows the peony, a traditional symbol of wealth, spring, and a sign of love and affection associated primarily with feminine beauty. The rose colored petals and the foliage are delicately shaded on a yellow gold ground. In logical sequence, the reverse side illustrates the chrysanthemum, an emblem of autumn and a sign of maturity with masculine implications. The side panels, echoing the motifs in the medallions, are on an aqua ground which complements the other tonalities. The neck has a rose colored key-fret motif and the base has the typical raised blue enamel inscription, *Qianlong nianzhi* (made in the Qianlong period). Height: 1 7/8 in. (4.7 cm)
Exhibited: Hong Kong Museum of Art. Catalogue, no. 20.
Illustrated: Stevens, op. cit., no. 965.

■ **100. ENAMELS ON GLASS 1736-1795—**
The double gourd shape has been used for many centuries as a symbol of fertility and longevity. This example is finely drawn illustrating prunus blossoms on bare branches with bamboo foliage on the lower half. The ground is citron yellow, brightly contrasting with the *famille rose* of the flowers. It includes the raised blue enamel inscription, *Qianlong nianzhi* (made in the Qianlong period). A thin blue line terminates the neck and the base. Height: 2 1/8 in. (5.4 cm)
Exhibited: Hong Kong Museum of Art. Catalogue, no. 25.
Illustrated: Stevens, op. cit., no. 968.
Illustrated: *Arts of Asia*, loc. cit., p. 37.

■ **101. ENAMELS ON GLASS 1736-1795—**
Another example of the palace workshop production is this fine polychromed bottle on milk glass. Each face has peonies and asters in medallions, with a contrasting citron yellow ground. The surround is a dull rose, with brilliant blue stylized flowers and leaf motifs adding contrast to the photographic detailing of flowers in the medallions. The neck has a lappet detail surrounding it and the base has the authentic raised blue enamel inscription, *Qianlong nianzhi* (made in the Qianlong period). Height: 2 1/8 in. (5.4 cm)
Formerly in the collection of Lilla S. Perry.
Illustrated: Stevens, op. cit., no. 964.

■ **102. ENAMELS ON GLASS 1736-1795—**
This miniature vessel of transparent golden yellow glass has a deeper palette of polychromed enamels than the preceding bottles. One face illustrates a rock on which a bird is perched looking up at a butterfly. The entire scene is surrounded by poppy blossoms in white, red, and green foliage. The reverse side illustrates hollyhock blossoms with asters and bamboo foliage. The neck has an unusual stylized floral band and the base has an authentic raised blue enamel inscription, *Qianlong nianzhi* (made in the Qianlong period). Height: 1 13/16 in. (4.5 cm)
Formerly in the collection of Russell Mullin.

■ **103. ENAMELS ON GLASS 1900-1965—**
While we again see a bottle that is stylistically eighteenth century in character, there is no mistaking the artist and period of this bottle, due solely to the research made by Hugh M. Moss. A member of the Ye family has put his seal in rose enamels at the end of a beautiful poem in standard script which reads: 'Sparse foliage gently reveals the thorns. Profuse blossoms gingerly hide the branches.' While translations of Chinese calligraphy are always inadequate, the picture rendered in this instance illustrates the beauty of the text with lovely peonies blossoming amid thorny branches. The reverse shows a plumed bird on a branch amid similar flowers and foliage. A highly stylized leaf and flower motif at the neck completes this elegant vessel. The Ye family made an untold number of bottles such as this, each with consummate skill and aesthetic merit. Height: 2 3/8 in. (6.0 cm)
See reverse illustration on page 75.
Illustrated: *Arts of Asia*, op. cit., col. pl., p. 34.

■ **104. ENAMELS ON GLASS 1825-1900—**
Opaque caramel colored glass is frequently seen carrying the iron red inscription *Guyuexuan* on the base as in this example. The flattened ovoid shape is enameled in *famille rose* colors depicting butterflies amid wild flowers with foliage and asters. The neck has a stylized lappet motif with tassels dropping from each trefoil. Height: 2 3/16 in. (5.6 cm)

■ **105. ENAMELS ON GLASS 1825-1900—**
Stylistically this bottle has many characteristics of eighteenth century design, but the colors and the type of painting are reminiscent of the Daoguang period and therefore is attributed to the nineteenth century. The flattened pear shape of opaque white glass is enameled in *famille rose* colors illustrating a grasshopper on a cabbage with asters nearby. The reverse side illustrates a turnip with another grasshopper and flowers adjacent. The neck has a lappet motif and from it drops a finely detailed necklace with tassels surrounding the bottle. The base has no inscription, another feature which helps confirm the nineteenth century dating for this bottle. Height: 2 1/4 in. (5.7 cm)

■ **106. ENAMELS ON GLASS 1790-1950—**
This delicate square vase tapering towards the bottom is finely enameled in *famille rose* colors on each face. The panels represent flowers of the seasons: prunus blossoms for winter, peony blossoms for spring, multicolored asters for summer, chrysanthemums for autumn. The base is inscribed with the traditional raised blue enamel seal, *Qianlong nianzhi* (made in the Qianlong period). The bottle may be of the period, but while the quality of the painting is fine, it differs from the preceding bottle which is closer to the style of other nineteenth century *Guyuexuan* bottles seen on this page. Thus, despite the seal, there is reason to believe that the Ye family in Beijing may have produced this particular example. Height: 2 9/16 in. (6.5 cm)

■ **107. ENAMELS ON GLASS 1800-1890—**
Finely decorated glass bottles were in great demand in the eighteenth and nineteenth centuries. This one has characteristics that reflect the cultural feeling of the eighteenth century, but style and use of color place it later. Each face illustrates an old gentleman playing with a group of boys in a rocky garden amid pine and bamboo trees. The symbols here are that of filial piety and gratitude. The base has a finely detailed raised blue enamel inscription, *Qianlong nianzhi* (made in the Qianlong period) but it is probably not of the period. Height: 2 1/4 in. (5.7 cm)

99

100

101

102

103

104

105

106

107

Description

■ **108. RUBY GLASS 1700-1800**—Simple glass bottles have been made since the earliest creation of snuff bottles. This flattened vase form of transparent ruby red coloring is beautifully contoured with a raised rim foot and finely carved masks with mock ring handles on the sides. The vessel also has an unusually wide mouth, which adds credence to the early date. Height: 1 15/16 in. (5.0 cm)

■ **109. IMPERIAL YELLOW GLASS 1750-1850**—The value of yellow seen here was truly the emperor's color during the Qing dynasty. Qianlong issued strict laws forbidding the use of yellow except for the imperial family. Following his reign, however, the color was used indiscriminately, making the task of dating these bottles quite difficult. This cylindrical shape is carved into eight panels in low relief with a lappet border near the neck and tassels dropping within each panel. The raised base and stopper have stylized lotus petals for decoration. The stopper is original in this instance, perfectly coordinating with the overall design. Height: 2 1/16 in. (5.1 cm)

■ **110. IMPERIAL YELLOW GLASS 1700-1780**—Scholars have noted that glass ingots were shipped to Beijing for carving in the lapidary technique. This example clearly can be related to the imperial workshops based on its design. Additionally, the surface indicates extensive use. The miniature shape is octagonal, with a medallion in the center of each multi-faceted side. This form was popular among the early carvers of bottles. Height: 1 9/16 in. (4.0 cm)

■ **111. BLUE GLASS 1700-1800**—Opaque glass was commonly used in the early period. This cobalt blue example reflects the characteristics of many in its category, including a very wide mouth, a high rim foot, and the presence of swirls within the context of the glass. In documents listing rare materials, opaque glass (*liuli*) was included along with semi-precious stones not indigenous to China. The bottle is attributed to the Beijing palace workshops although there is no seal on the base. Height: 2 1/16 in. (5.1 cm)

■ **112. SPECKLED GLASS 1720-1820**—This transparent dark blue glass is not only dignified by a beautiful shape but by copper filings mixed within the context of the molten material at some point before blowing or molding. The neck of the bottle possesses an unusually wide mouth. Again, this type of vessel was found in the early period of snuff bottle making but continued into the nineteenth century. Height: 2 1/8 in. (5.4 cm)

■ **113. SPECKLED ORANGE GLASS 1720-1820**—The Chinese of the eighteenth century were enamored of a striking orange red mineral called realgar. However, it could not be easily used for practical purposes because, as arsenic ore, the material is poisonous and in fact is very soft. Realgar became one of the materials most ingeniously imitated in glass throughout the snuff bottle making period. This example, with its highly contrasting red to orange splotches on a caramel ground, is one of the earlier bottles as shown by the character of the neck, its concavity, and its width. Height: 2 7/16 in. (6.2 cm)

■ **114. SWIRL GLASS 1730-1830**—It is believed that glass of the type seen here was sent in ingots of various colors from Boshan in Shandong Province to Beijing for melting and working. This example, with its modern abstract design of darting, swirling red and yellow lines, derives its colors from metallic oxides mixed in plain glass. While this bottle is thought to be from the early period, the type continued to be made throughout the nineteenth century. Height: 1 15/16 in. (5.0 cm)

■ **115. MILK GLASS 1700-1800**—This pure flattened vase form is completely undecorated. The bottle's distinction lies in its perfection of shape and purity of color, which in truth is absence of color. Not discernible in the photograph, the base is carved in a concave manner adding subtle character to this early vessel—truly the taste of the Chinese literati. Height: 2 1/4 in. (5.8 cm)

■ **116. AMBER GLASS 1700-1790**—It appears that Chinese glassmakers were constantly competing with each other to devise new ways of making innovative bottle textures and styles. This elongated vessel of transparent amber glass has soft white splotches interspersed around the entire surface. The simplicity of the form, its color, the foot, and the neck, all help confirm an eighteenth century date. Height: 3 in. (7.5 cm)

■ **117. IMPERIAL YELLOW GLASS 1736-1795**—In this instance, the finely incised four-character inscription, *Qianlong nianzhi* (made in the Qianlong period), on the base of the bottle, confirms that the color here is indeed imperial yellow. This spade-shaped vessel is finely carved and full of symbolic meaning. One face illustrates a quail under a millet plant and on the reverse is a butterfly approaching a turnip. These symbols imply courage and perseverance as well as abundance. The sides and neck are carved in a hexagonal diaper pattern. Height: 1 7/8 in. (4.8 cm)

108
109
110
111
112
113
114
115
116
117

Description

■ **118. OVERLAY GLASS 1720-1820**—The Chinese name for overlay glass is *taoliao*. The technique did not originate with the Chinese but more likely in Egypt and later Europe. Ruby red overlay on a camphor glass ground has been among the most popular combinations of glass bottle makers. On one face, we see a tiered palace and its fortification surrounded by water. The opposite side shows a pyramid-shaped building rising miraculously from the clouds which emanate from swirling waters. On each face, the felicitous bat of happiness hovers above. The sides are uniquely detailed with highly stylized standing rocks. A red overlay of churning waves covers part of the base of this early bottle. Height: 2 1/4 in. (5.8 cm)

■ **119. OVERLAY GLASS 1750-1850**—Single color overlay on a blown or molded glass bottle was the most common technique throughout the eighteenth and nineteenth centuries. This example of cobalt blue on a vitreous milky white ground shows two five-clawed dragons wrapped around the vessel seeking the flaming pearl on the upper part of one shoulder. At the bottom is a strong wave motif. The perfect delineation of the design against the finely polished ground is the distinguishing feature of this bottle. Another detail, which cannot be seen in the photograph, is the overlay carved blue two-character seal on the base. Only one of the characters can be read with certainty, *zhi*. It is probably part of the maker's name. Height: 2 7/16 in. (6.2 cm)
Formerly in the collection of Ralph M. Hults.

■ **120. OVERLAY GLASS 1720-1800**—Amber colored glass such as the example seen here was often created to simulate amber. The unusual feature of this bottle is that one face shows an overlay of slightly iridescent coloring, carved in deep relief to show thinly gnarled branches with blossoms. The opposite side, in dramatic contrast, has a prominent relief design of medallion form illustrating Shoulao with an unusually large staff walking by a pavilion under a pine tree near a rocky mountain. The weight of the glass, suggesting a heavy lead content, and the style of the carving lead us to attribute this bottle to the Beijing palace workshops. Height: 2 1/4 in. (5.7 cm)

■ **121. OVERLAY GLASS 1730-1830**—The basic bottle in this instance is of clear amber coloration with a heavy overlay emanating from the bottom and tapering toward the top in a caramel tone detailed to illustrate a stylized dragon on each face. Dominant wave patterns surround the entire lower area and wrap around the base of the vessel. Again, a slightly pitted overlay surface and a very wide mouth indicate an early date. Height: 2 7/8 in. (7.3 cm)

■ **122. OVERLAY GLASS 1750-1840**—This spade-shaped bottle has a caramel colored ground with a rich jade green overlay. The carving is a fanciful design showing a grasshopper on one side and on the reverse a praying mantis feasting on top of snow pea pods. The foliage and tendrils continue in a running pattern around the bottle. The definition of the design and the sharpness of the carving are particularly fine. Height: 2 1/2 in. (6.4 cm)

■ **123. OVERLAY GLASS 1800-1900**—This vessel illustrates the 'Hundred Antiquities' which are drawn from archaic bronze forms of the Shang and Zhou dynasties. The term implies a multiplicity of objects, most of which could be labeled family treasures. In all, nine independent vessels are detailed in an amber colored overlay on a citron yellow ground, a most unusual combination. Height: 2 3/4 in. (7.0 cm)

■ **124. OVERLAY GLASS 1760-1860**—Glass with bubbles induced in the molten stage has been given various names such as camphor, snowflake, or snowstorm. This elongated vase shape includes six colors overlaid on an amber 'snowflake' ground. The design suggests a lotus pond with nine fantail goldfish swirling around the bottle with lotus blossoms near the top. In multicolored single overlay bottles such as this example, the various hues are applied in localized areas by the use of tubes, each of a different color. Height:. 3 1/8 in. (7.9 cm)

■ **125. OVERLAY GLASS 1750-1840**—If one wishes to differentiate between camphor glass and snowflake glass, this bottle would seem to be camphor as opposed to the snowflake ground seen on previous bottles. The scene depicted is of the eight horses of Mu Wang, the fifth king of the Zhou dynasty whose chariot was led by eight resplendent horses. Each horse illustrated on the bottle is rendered in a deep cobalt blue overlay. The horse, domesticated in China since the Shang dynasty, was a symbol of rank, power, and wealth. In this vessel, the horses have special animation related to body movement which immediately demonstrates their symbolic meaning. Height: 2 7/16 in. (6.2 cm)
Illustrated: *Newsletter*, June 1973, p. 10, fig. 20.
Illustrated: *JICSBS*, June 1976, p. 16, fig. 7.

■ **126. OVERLAY GLASS 1820-1900**—This bulbous shape with a finely speckled camphor ground is differentiated from the preceding bottles by a dull-finish blue overlay of enamel paste squeezed on with a pointed instrument, as opposed to the carving of overlay glass. Its other unusual feature is the use of the eight precious Buddhist emblems to decorate the surface. Four are shown on each side: the conch shell, the umbrella, the endless knot, and the wheel of the law on one side; the lotus, the precious vase, the fish, and the canopy on the other. Height: 2 1/2 in. (6.4 cm)
Illustrated: *Newsletter*, June 1973, p. 6, fig. 7.

■ **127. IMPERIAL YELLOW GLASS 1750-1820**—Bottles of this type are attributed to the Beijing palace workshops because of their overall style, the quality of the carving, as well as the texture and tone of the glass. In this example, we see a repetition of the symbols of longevity and emolument, with a crane under a pine tree on one side and a deer under a pine on the reverse. However, the design runs continuously around the vessel in elegant refinement, all emanating from a rocky garden base. Height: 2 1/2 in. (6.4 cm)
Illustrated: *Arts of Asia, op. cit.*, p. 32

118 119 120

121 122 123 124

125 126 127

Description

■ **128. OVERLAY GLASS 1820-1900**—The camphor glass example seen here is a true double overlay. The first slip is of a mossy green tonality overlaid with a rust red color. The face of this vessel illustrates flowering orchids with butterflies, and the familiar *lingzhi* is seen near the base. The foliage on the opposite side is a carved bamboo tree emanating from a rocky garden, and above we see a bird feeding baby chicks on the branches. Height: 2 3/16 in. (5.5 cm)

■ **129. OVERLAY GLASS 1800-1900**—Many symbols and pictorial details distinguish this bottle of ruby red overlay on a snowflake ground. The face reveals a rendering of a quotation from the *Yijing, The Book of Changes*, where we find it under the first hexagram which denotes the creative power of heaven. The quotation beautifully describes the dragon on the opposite side and reads: 'The dragon is flying in the sky, it is opportune to see personages in high positions. The characters are detailed in high relief. The noted scholar, Max Loehr, tells us that 'the flavor of antiquity in this passage from one of the oldest Chinese Classics combines with the no less ancient style of writing in the monumental Chou seal characters to endow this piece with an irresistible air of ancientness.' The reverse side shows the highly spirited five-clawed imperial dragon also carved in high relief. The sides of the vessel are decorated with the eight Daoist emblems including a fan, a flower basket, a lotus, a sword, castanets, a flute, and a bamboo tube. The base includes another relief carving of a four-character seal of the Shunzhi emperor (the first of the Qing emperors, 1644-1661). Everything about this bottle is honorific, including the inscription; therefore it is unlikely that a bottle of this style would have been fashioned in the beginning of the snuff bottle period. Height: 2 9/16 in. (6.9 cm)
Illustrated: *Newsletter*, June 1973, p. 5, fig. 1.
For a discussion of the bottle see p. 4.

■ **130. OVERLAY GLASS 1820-1920**—Color is the distinguishing feature of this purse-shaped bottle of deep transparent green tonality with an opaque cinnabar red overlay. One face shows the famous scene depicting He Xiangu with her flower basket, rowing a log canoe in rough waters. The reverse side illustrates the setting sun falling into turbulent waters with a crane flying above. The underside is carved to show the origin of the waves swirling in different directions. The economical use of color on this bottle dramatizes the cameo quality of the carver's technique. Height: 2 3/16 in. (5.6 cm)
Illustrated: *Newsletter*, June 1973, p. 9, fig. 14.

■ **131. OVERLAY GLASS 1800-1880**—A snowflake glass ground is again used as a foil for a dramatic red and black overlay bottle. One face illustrates a deer and a stork with a branch of *lingzhi* in his mouth from the plant nearby. They are prime symbols of longevity and emolument, under the ever-present pine tree. The reverse side shows magpies on the branches of a blossoming prunus tree. The overall theme is one of happiness and long life. Height: 2 7/8 in. (7.3 cm)
Illustrated: *Arts of Asia, op. cit.*, col. pl., p. 34.

■ **132. OVERLAY GLASS 1750-1850**—The flattened vase form of this ruby red bottle is highlighted by imperial yellow overlay. The face shows an elegant scholar's seal with a Buddhist lion on top; the square base is rendered in two dimensions with the side panel revealing the inscription, *Wenshan ke*, meaning 'carved by Wenshan.' The reverse side shows finely carved characters in seal script referring to the establishment of a royal library. The inscription can be translated: 'Collecting books under the constellations *Dong* and *Bi*; scholars gathering in the West Garden.' The side panels show a pair of hydras climbing up the bottle on one side and down on the other. Height: 2 13/16 in. (7.2 cm)
See reverse illustration on page 75.

■ **133. OVERLAY GLASS 1820-1900**—One of the most extensively used symbols in Chinese art is that of the *fo* dog, or Buddhist lion. The camphor ground bottle with true double overlay details four differing postures of the lion-dog, one on each face and one on each side. The animal is dominant in appearance as a true protector of the faith and is a symbol of valor and energy. His curly mane, and forked tail, and broad jaw add strength to his visage. Here, he is playing with the famous brocaded ball which, as frequently seen, is beribboned with flowing sashes spreading over the bottle. Height: 2 9/16 in. (6.5 cm)
Illustrated: *Newsletter*, June 1973, p. 13, fig. 27.
Illustrated: *JICSBS*, June 1976, p. 16, fig. 6.

■ **134. OVERLAY GLASS 1740-1840**—Lustrous milk glass is a dramatic foil for a jet black overlay. The artist has detailed this vessel with a delicacy appropriate to the scene of the three friends: the prunus, the pine, and the bamboo. The three friends motif has been used over many centuries to symbolize qualities of faithfulness, companionship, and loyalty. These attributes sometimes indicate the relationship between the maker and the receiver of such a bottle. Height: 2 1/2 in. (6.4 cm)

■ **135. OVERLAY GLASS Dated 1884**—Single overlay bottles are frequently of multicolors, as in this example. The five color design is carved to illustrate seven fantail goldfish in a lotus pond—a very fanciful rendering. One upper side shows the cyclical date, made in 1884. Height: 2 1/2 in. (6.4 cm)

■ **136. OVERLAY GLASS 1850-1930**—True triple overlays are relatively rare and this example of the water buffalo and the boy with a kite is a good example. A simple flattened vase of transparent glass clearly illustrates three distinct overlays on a camphor ground. The first layer, of yellow, is at the neck and is also used for highlighting throughout the bottle. The second layer, of grassy green, forms the figures and bodies as well as the sky. The third layer, of cinnabar red, serves as an accent tonality for faces, flowers, and other details. The ox or water buffalo typifies the overladen peasant. An appropriately secular touch is provided by the small detail of the herd boy's flying kite. Height: 2 1/2 in. (6.3 cm)
Illustrated: *Newsletter*, June 1973, p. 12, fig. 23.

■ **137. OVERLAY GLASS 1850-1930**—It is felt that the majority of seal-type overlay glass bottles were produced in Yangzhou in the second half of the nineteenth century and well into the twentieth century. This example of pure milk glass with a black overlay represents the school at its best. The sharply detailed design illustrates the daring movement of an elderly bearded fisherman under a tree on one side; the reverse shows a cat looking at butterflies amid flowers and branches. The seal in the upper corner identifies the subjects as symbols of old age. The scene also alludes to the yin and yang theme—the cat being the yin or passive female symbol and the butterflies the active male counterparts. The sides have animal masks with long mock ring handles. Height: 2 3/16 in. (5.6 cm)
See reverse illustration on page 75.
Formerly in the collection of Lilla S. Perry.
Illustrated: Perry, *op cit.*, p. 48, no. 14.

128
129
130
131
132
133
134
135
136
137

Description

■ **138. EMBELLISHED GLASS 1800-1900**—Embellished vessels were made throughout the snuff bottle making period, but this particular example belongs to the nineteenth century. The vessel is ovoid in shape and of an opaque turquoise blue color with a rim foot. The embellishment on each side is of iridescent mother-of-pearl shell meticulously applied to show a typical Chinese garden landscape with flowering trees and birds. A fierce mask is mounted on each shoulder. Height: 1 15/16 in. (5.0 cm)
See reverse illustration on page 75.
Formerly in the collection of Arthur Loveless.
Illustrated: Perry, op. cit., p. 146, no. 160.
Illustrated: Arts of Asia, op. cit., col. pl., p. 34.

■ **139. INCISED GLASS Dated 1845**—A few incised milky white glass bottles belong to a distinct group of vessels carved by known artists, some of which are dated. All are of the nineteenth century. One face shows a finely drawn pair of horses under a willow tree. The opposite side reveals a charming poem about lovers, finely written in seal script. The text reads as follows:

> The bright moon is rising from the sea,
> Even if we are separated, we can share
>   this moment.
> The lovers are separated far away,
> Tonight they miss each other.

The artist who rendered this calligraphy and the scene on the opposite side is named on the lower left corner of the bottle, Cheng Ziqing. Height: 2 1/2 in. (6.4 cm)

■ **140. OVERLAY GLASS 1830-1900**—This particular bottle has special character because the seal on each side, written in standard script, identifies the historic scene depicted. One face speaks of General Su Wu shepherding his sheep. We see the famous general in exile, seated under a pine tree watching the grazing sheep. The reverse shows the familiar subject of an old man on a mule followed by a boy, under prunus blossoms. The seal reads: 'Treading the snow looking for plum blossoms.' The soft transparent blue bottle is carved with a tinted white overlay revealing true cameo-style carving. Height: 2 7/16 in. (6.1 cm)

■ **141. EMBELLISHED GLASS 1820-1900**—Chinese craftsmen delighted in simulating other materials in the medium of glass. The striations in the glass here suggest chalcedony or agate. It is only through scratching the base that the author was convinced that the material could be none other than glass. The embellishment on the vessel is equally distinguished because of its lightness and delicacy. The minerals used to create this spring-like scene of flowers and branches include malachite, coral, lapis lazuli, amethyst, turquoise, and carnelian. The bottle is probably earlier than the decoration. Height: 2 7/16 in. (6.1 cm)
Illustrated: JICSBS, March 1976, p. 6.

■ **142. OVERLAY GLASS 1750-1800**—The four-color single overlay bottle seen here is of opaque milk glass. We again observe the four seasons illustrated in the prunus blossoms of spring, the peonies of summer, the chrysanthemum of autumn, and the bamboo of winter. Each flower is rendered in a different tonality: green, rose, blue, and gold. The entire outer base is carved in rockery with a rim foot below. The definition of the design, the cutting, and the polishing of the surface are all hallmarks of early overlay glass. Height: 2 9/16 in. (6.8 cm)

■ **143. EMBELLISHED GLASS 1820-1900**—The same studio that created bottle no. 141 more than likely produced this elegant vessel. The completely transparent soft, sea green tone adds brilliance to the appliqués of mother-of-pearl, coral, jasper, and malachite. The scene is of birds and butterflies hovering over bunches of grapes falling from graceful branches and foliage. The shoulders include fierce masks with mock ring handles in applied mother-of-pearl. Height: 2 1/2 in. (6.3 cm)

■ **144. OVERLAY GLASS 1800-1900**—This caparisoned elephant is carved of double overlay glass on a white ground showing the body in a bright pink and the head and trappings, with a large bat, in dark green. The side panels also include the bat, symbol of happiness, and long tassels that are finely detailed as well as a *ruyi* motif near the neck of the bottle. Height: 2 7/8 in. (7.3 cm)
Illustrated: Arts of Asia, op. cit., col. pl., p. 35.

■ **145. OVERLAY GLASS 1830-1900**—Color is the distinguishing feature of this silhouette design. The rich rose ground is the foil for the dark shiny black overlay carved to illustrate a man playing a flute under a prunus blossom tree with the full moon above. The reverse side shows an equally spare scene with a young man brushing his favorite horse under a leafless tree. Adjacent to the horse's head is a four-character seal which reads *zhuangxin qianli*, meaning, 'Traveling one thousand miles with a stout heart.' The shoulders of the vessel are replete with masks and mock ring handles. Height: 2 5/16 in. (5.9 cm)

■ **146. OVERLAY GLASS 1720-1820**—This beautiful flattened vase form is typical of the early overlay types with a ground of speckled swirl patterns in rose, pink, and white. A thick white overlay is deeply carved forming the rocky base from which grow peony branches and blossoms terminating in pink. Height: 2 7/8 in. (7.3 cm)

138

139

140

141

142

143

144

145

146

Description

■ 147. BLUE AND WHITE PORCELAIN 1800-1880—Cylinder-shaped vessels of blue and white underglaze are common in the porcelain category. This example illustrates the dragon seeking the flaming pearl on one side with the mythical phoenix on the reverse. The base includes a finely drawn four-character inscription, *Yongzheng nianzhi* (made in the Yongzheng period). The site of the imperial kilns was at Jingdezhen in Jiangxi Province throughout the Ming and Qing dynasties except for short periods of insurrection. While many bottles bear the same four characters related to the Yongzheng period, most of them, including this one, were manufactured in the nineteenth century. Height: 2 1/8 in. (5.4 cm)

■ 148. BLUE AND WHITE PORCELAIN 1825-1900—The vase form is undoubtedly one of the most ubiquitous shapes in all of Chinese ceramic art. This cobalt blue on white example was painted under glaze in a bold manner illustrating the phoenix, symbol of the empress, on one side and the dragon, symbol of the emperor, on the opposite side. The balance of the composition is rendered in varying forms of cloud motifs. The base has a six-character inscription of the Yongzheng emperor, *Yongzheng nianzhi* (made in the Yongzheng period), but it is not of the period. Height: 2 9/16 in. (6.9 cm)

■ 149. ENAMELED PORCELAIN 1780-1850—Graceful double-gourd shapes abound in all categories of snuff bottles. This example is enameled using *famille rose* colors in a pattern which is traditionally called millefleurs. The quality of the painting as well as the colors strongly suggest an eighteenth century date, though the bottle could have been made as late as the first half of the nineteenth century. The base is inscribed in red enamel, *Qianlong nianzhi* (made in the Qianlong period) in seal script which has almost vanished. Height: 2 3/16 in. (5.5 cm)
Formerly in the collection of Mrs. Elmer A. Claar.
Illustrated: Stevens, *op. cit.*, no. 300.

■ 150. PORCELAIN 1740-1800—The example seen here is a baluster-form porcelain from the imperial kilns at Jingdezhen. The unusual feature of this bottle is in the *rose du Barry* glaze which covers the entire surface and is etched in a highly stylized vine pattern. Superimposed are flowers and branches in *famille rose* colors that relate in style and color to the eighteenth century. The base has an iron red four-character mark in seal script, *Qianlong nianzhi* (made in the Qianlong period). Height: 2 9/16 in. (6.5 cm)
Formerly in the collection of Martin Schoen.
Illustrated: *JICSBS*, March 1975, front cover.
Illustrated: *JICSBS*, March 1980, p. 7, fig. 11.

■ 151. MOLDED PORCELAIN 1780-1820—This large porcelain bottle from the imperial factory is covered with a milky white glaze. The mold details the famous eighteen Luohans, each with his familiar attribute, or animal, on a wave pattern ground. The severity of the white is relieved by a flaming iron red pearl near the neck. It is interesting to note the similarity between this bottle and the soapstone bottle of the same subject, no. 38. Height: 2 7/8 in. (7.3 cm)
Exhibited: Hong Kong Museum of Art. Catalogue, no. 108.
Illustrated: *Newsletter*, June 1973, p. 6, fig. 6.
Illustrated: *JICSBS*, March 1980, p. 6, fig. 4.

■ 152. MOLDED PORCELAIN 1780-1820—An unusual example of a vase form molded and refined in high relief is seen here. The artist shows a dragon with open jaws and details distinctive enough to see the great animal's teeth. The flaming pearl is rendered in gold. The opposite side illustrates a phoenix bird in a celestial garden. A ground of dull gray blue tone is enlivened by clouds and *lingzhi* plants —emblems of immortality. Height: 2 3/4 in. (7.0 cm)
See reverse illustration on page 75.
Formerly in the collection of Lilla S. Perry.
Illustrated: Perry, *op. cit.*, p. 80, no. 60.
Illustrated: *Arts of Asia, op. cit.*, p. 32.
Illustrated: *JICSBS*, March 1980, p. 6, fig. 4.
Illustrated: *JICSBS*, June 1980, p. 15.
Illustrated: *JICSBS*, December 1981, p. 26, no. 41.

■ 153. MONOCHROME PORCELAIN 1780-1850—This bulbous bottle has an unusual glaze called teadust by Chinese connoisseurs. The dark mossy green vertical striations suggest a fur-like texture. The glaze was invented for imperial use in the eighteenth century, but was used occasionally in the nineteenth century. Height: 2 3/16 in. (5.5 cm)
Formerly in the collections of Georgia Roode and Lilla S. Perry.

■ 154. MOLDED PORCELAIN 1780-1820—The imperial factory at Jingdezhen could be the only source for this soft-paste porcelain bottle of classic form, molded to ultimate refinement. The ground area is sharply defined in a wave motif and the figures are undercut, giving a three-dimensional aspect to the bottle. Each of the eighteen Luohans amid the clouds is depicted, with his vehicle and attribute, with an expressiveness that could almost be described as portraiture. The ground is flat in texture but the raised surfaces are all glazed in an eggshell tone. The base does not have a reign mark but this quality could only be found at the imperial levels. Height: 2 9/16 in. (6.9 cm)
Illustrated: *Newsletter*, September 1972, p. 3.
Illustrated: *Newsletter*, June 1973, p. 6, fig. 5.

■ 155. MONOCHROME PORCELAIN 1790-1880—This molded-flask shape with a dull gold crackled glaze is undecorated except for masks on each shoulder with mock ring handles in a dull brown tone. The unusual characteristic of this bottle is a dark brown underglaze inscription *Guyuexuan*. The use of this studio name along with the mellow texture and the concave mouth of the bottle adds some credence for an early date, though the style continued throughout the nineteenth century. Height: 2 5/8 in. (6.6 cm)

147

148

149

150

151

152

153

154

155

Description

■ **156. ENAMELED PORCELAIN 1796-1820**—An elegantly enameled spade-shaped bottle shows a young court lady holding a *ruyi* scepter as an attendant presents peaches in a bowl. They stand on the terrace with a mountain landscape in the background. On the reverse, the two have moved to another point in the same garden and this time the lady holds a precious blue vase and the attendant holds the *ruyi* scepter. Each of these panels is surrounded on the sides and the neck by stylized floral and branch motifs in multicolors on a rose background. The original matching stopper is still with the vessel. The base is inscribed in iron red, *Jiaqing nianzhi* (made in the Jiaqing period) in seal script. Height: 2 5/8 in. (6.6 cm)

■ **157. ENAMELED PORCELAIN 1796-1820**—Each face of this ovoid vessel is decorated in *famille rose* colors on a milky ground. The flowers are peonies and asters with delicate foliage and the panels surrounding the medallions are again of stylized floral and branch motifs on a chartreuse ground. The base is incised in iron red, *Jiaqing nianzhi* (made in the Jiaqing period). Height: 2 1/8 in. (5.4 cm)
Formerly in the collection of Lilla S. Perry.
Exhibited: Hong Kong Museum of Art. Catalogue, no. 112.
Illustrated: Perry, *op. cit.*, p. 85, no. 67.
Illustrated: *JICSBS*, March 1975, front cover.
Illustrated: *Arts of Asia, op. cit.*, p. 37.
Illustrated: *JICSBS*, March 1980, p. 7, fig. 8.

■ **158. ENAMELED PORCELAIN 1796-1820**—This simple vase shape is decorated with a famous scene in which twenty magpies rest on a blossoming prunus tree. Since magpies are symbols of good luck and happiness, twenty should bring more fortune than enough. Soft *famille rose* colors on a white ground are an appropriate setting for this evocation of spring. The base of the bottle has a four-character iron red reign mark of Jiaqing. Height: 2 13/16 in. (7.1 cm)
Illustrated: *Newsletter*, June 1973, p. 12, fig. 26.
Illustrated: *JICSBS*, June 1976, p. 17, fig. 19.

■ **159. MOLDED PORCELAIN 1796-1820**—Some designs are seen frequently, but in varying degrees of quality. This example brings together all of the qualities that constitute an imperial product. The nine Buddhist lions are playing with the big brocaded and beribboned balls with an energy that can only be described as competitive. The enameling adds much to the beauty of the vessel as well as the undercutting and reticulated work between surfaces and the aqua tone ground. The neck and base have the traditional lappet motif, with the key-fret pattern at the upper part of the neck. The base is inscribed with the traditional *Jiaqing nianzhi* (made in the Jiaqing period). Height: 2 5/8 in. (6.6 cm)

■ **160. MOLDED PORCELAIN 1850-1900**—The fanciful cabbage shape is venerated by the Chinese as a symbol of plenty. An otherwise common mold is characterized by refinement of leaf detail and foliage and thinness of texture. The enamel decoration in tones of aqua, green, and white is judiciously used. Height: 2 13/16 in. (7.1 cm)

■ **161. MOLDED PORCELAIN 1796-1820**—Jingdezhen is again the source of this atypical mold. Polychromed enamels in *famille rose* colors on a white glazed ground delineate a continuous scene of lotus blossoms with figures in boats plucking flowers. The reverse side shows two figures in a pavilion amid a rocky garden. The base is inscribed in red, *Jiaqing nianzhi* (made in the Jiaqing period) in seal script. Height: 2 1/2 in. (6.3 cm)

■ **162. MOLDED PORCELAIN 1800-1860**—An unusual form of double bottle or twin-necked design is molded in *famille rose* colors on a gold ground. On one face we see a bountiful domestic scene with playful ladies in a garden scene outside a finely detailed interior space with a tile roof. On the reverse is a grand gathering of officials and generals before a high personage, as if in convocation. Among the more fanciful Qing dynasty porcelain forms, this vessel is unmarked on the base except for the gilding. Height: 2 5/8 in. (6.6 cm)
Illustrated: *JICSBS*, March 1975, front cover.

156

157

158

159

160

161

162

Description

■ **163. PORCELAIN 1790-1860**—The *shou* (longevity) character has been used in symbolic and calligraphic form for hundreds of years. This spade-shaped vessel of white porcelain is decorated in red enamel with one hundred different calligraphic forms of the same character. The stylization is executed with great imagination and diversity. The iron red borders and neck depict stylized leaf and flower motifs while remnants of gold still outline each medallion. The base has the traditional four-character Qianlong mark in red but the overall character of the bottle indicates that it was produced in the nineteenth century, rather than in the century of the emperor named. Height: 2 1/8 in. (5.4 cm)

■ **164. PORCELAIN 1800-1880**—If the general quality of a bottle is an indication of age, this one should be from the imperial kiln and of the Qianlong period as marked on its base; but that is not the case. Renderings of the eight horses are among the most common in all of Chinese pictorial art. Mu Wang, the fifth sovereign of the Zhou dynasty, made famous the horses which drew his great chariot and his name is among the most distinguished and venerated of emperors. The depiction here is romantic and convivial, as the horses appear to be making love; and if color is an additive to that mood, the *famille rose* colors are perfect for the scene. Masks and mock ring handles, and a blue key-fret motif at the base are complemented by the lappet motif around the neck. Height: 2 3/16 in. (5.5 cm)

■ **165. PORCELAIN 1800-1880**—Another example of elegantly decorated porcelain, with the imperial mark of the Qianlong emperor on the base. The overall character of the bottle, however, and the number of bottles known to exist of the same design, would probably place it in the nineteenth century. The eighteen Luohans in this setting enjoy themselves in a verdant landscape; all is detailed in *famille rose* colors on a burnished gold ground. Height: 2 3/16 in. (5.5 cm)
Illustrated: *JICSBS*, June 1976, p. 16, fig. 9.

■ **166. MOLDED PORCELAIN 1800-1860**—An interesting example is seen here of a double walled, reticulated porcelain in soft blue that resembles the *clair de lune* glaze. In this instance, the powerful five-clawed dragon which dominates one face is sharply defined including bulging black eyes. The reverse side shows the flaming pearl which here eludes the dragon. Height: 2 7/16 in. (6.1 cm)

■ **167. MOLDED PORCELAIN 1796-1850**—A miniature bulbous shape has a continuous design of five bats amid the clouds on a raised and stippled aqua tone ground. While there is no reign mark on the base, the bottle shows gradations of color and stylistic detail which resemble late eighteenth century work. More than likely, however, it is another example of the finesse in molded porcelain of the nineteenth century. The decoration is a rebus for the saying *wufu linmen*, meaning, 'May the five blessings visit you.' Height: 1 5/8 in. (4.1 cm)
Illustrated: *Newsletter*, December 1973, p. 12, fig. 4.

■ **168. PORCELAIN 1800-1880**—This medallion-shaped vessel is enameled with a miniature circle motif in iron red as a ground on which is a stylized flower and branch motif in *famille rose* colors. The entire border and neck are in underglaze cobalt blue, again of stylized floral and leaf motifs. The Qianlong underglaze blue four-character mark is on the base but it is probably not of the period. Height: 2 7/16 in. (6.1 cm)

■ **169. MOLDED PORCELAIN 1790-1850**—The Eight Immortals are legendary beings from the Daoist tradition, though three are historical personages. They correspond to the eighteen Luohans of Buddhism but have different symbolic meanings. In this vessel, we see each of the figures with the attributes with which they perform miracles. It is also said that they can cross rivers and seas as easily as sentient beings walk on land. The *famille rose* colors add particular vivacity to this vessel. The base has the four-character reign mark of the Qianlong emperor. Height: 2 1/4 in. (5.8 cm)

■ **170. PORCELAIN 1800-1880**—Calligraphy is both theme and decoration for this vase-shaped vessel painted in underglaze cobalt blue. Around the neck of the bottle are four characters which give the actual title to a long poem in twelve lines of calligraphy running continuously around the bottle. The subject matter is plum blossoms in springtime. The base has the four-character reign mark of the Qianlong emperor but again the piece is more than likely honorific rather than of the period. Height: 2 13/16 in. (7.2 cm)
Illustrated: *Newsletter*, June 1973, p. 5, fig. 2.

■ **171. PORCELAIN 1821-1850**—This pear-shaped vessel of pure white porcelain is decorated to reveal a short poem, translated: 'The gentle breezes and the warm sun hasten to open the embroidered curtain. A pair of butterflies fly away but soon return home.' On the side with the calligraphy, we see the butterflies departing and on the reverse side two have returned to a resting place amid foliage and flowers in *famille rose* colors. The base has an iron red four-character inscription of the Daoguang emperor. Height: 2 7/16 in. (6.1 cm)

163

164

165

166

167

168

169

170

171

Description

■ **172. PORCELAIN 1821-1850**—Genuine Daoguang snuff bottles are not uncommon. This cylindrical shape, tapering toward the neck, is an imperial bottle with the genuine mark of the emperor in a grayish underglaze on the base. A pair of rampant five-clawed dragons in underglaze cobalt blue seek the flaming pearl. Interspersed over the bottle are flame motifs as well as clouds. The flaming pearl is almost within the grasp of each dragon, and yet eludes them. Height: 3 1/4 in. (8.2 cm)
Illustrated: *JICSBS*, March 1980, p. 8, fig. 14.

■ **173. PORCELAIN 1821-1850**—This cylindrical-shaped vessel is distinguished by its drawing in sepia tones on a background enameled in *famille noire*. The scene is a traditional landscape with two gentlemen departing their home for a long journey. A feeling of nostalgia is evoked as the first rider crosses the bridge near a weeping willow tree. The base has the traditional four-character mark of the Daoguang emperor in iron red. Height: 2 9/16 in. (6.5 cm)

■ **174. PORCELAIN 1820-1900**—We see another cylindrical bottle with the same subject as no. 172. In this example, the raging dragons are in iron red glaze, which adds a higher degree of drama than the blue and white bottle. While the base does not have an imperial reign mark, the design has the strength and virility one associates with the ageless dragon theme. Height: 3 1/8 in. (8.0 cm)
Illustrated: *JICSBS*, June 1976, p. 16, fig. 2.

■ **175. MOLDED AND CARVED PORCELAIN 1800-1850**—The next two bottles are likely to be products of the Jingdezhen imperial factory that produced this type of porcelain over a period of a hundred years. This flattened vase form bears the molded raised characters of the artist, Wang Bingrong. The artist was one of the few early nineteenth century carvers to use his name, and later in the century others are known to have copied his work. The delicate landscape scene illustrates houseboats in the water against a pine-covered mountain backdrop. The opposite side continues the mountain and water theme with two men in a sampan. A pale celadon glaze adds particular beauty to this example. Height: 2 9/16 in. (6.9 cm)
Illustrated: *JICSBS*, March 1975, front cover.

■ **176. MOLDED AND CARVED PORCELAIN 1820-1880**—Another master carver fashioned this bottle with high relief detailing of trees and foliage amid a rural setting with mountains and pine trees. The opposite side shows a lone fisherman in a boat. The caramel color glaze adds depth to this distinctive scene. The base includes an incised four-character inscription which cannot be deciphered. Height: 2 13/16 in. (7.1 cm)

■ **177. YIXING 1800-1880**—Yixing stoneware was first made in the town by the same name on the western shore of Lake Taihu in Jiangsu Province. This earthenware is thought to date no earlier than the sixteenth century, but it is venerated among the Chinese and Japanese, especially for use in the tea ceremony. An atypical example of Yixing is seen in this flattened vase form. The dull off-white ground silhouettes two playful dogs. Shaggy brown hair is characteristically rendered to illustrate a bushy-tailed mother countenancing her puppy. Height: 2 5/16 in. (5.9 cm)

■ **178. YIXING 1700-1800**—Vessels such as this were definitely used in the eighteenth century. This charcoal black pottery vessel is carved in a continuous design with a basket-weave pattern bordered by two types of keyfret motifs. The base is impressed with the two-character seal, *zhi lan* (fungi and orchids). Height: 2 3/8 in. (6.0 cm)
Formerly in the collection of Martin Schoen.
Exhibited: China Institute. Catalogue, no. 98.
Exhibited: Hong Kong Museum of Art. Catalogue, no. 119.
Illustrated: *JICSBS*, September 1978, front cover.
Illustrated: *JICSBS*, March 1980, p. 8, fig. 16.

■ **179. YIXING 1780-1870**—Yixing ware was especially valued because of its ability to hold the flavor and freshness of the snuff. This ovoid bottle with round neck and rim foot is finished in a crackled, dull rose beige tone. The enameling on each face is of a free-style mountain landscape with a pavilion in tones of blue, green, and brown. Height: 2 7/16 in. (6.1 cm)

172

173

174

175

176

177

178

179

Description

■ **180. INSIDE-PAINTED GLASS** by Gan Huan, dated 1825. The only known early school artist, Gan Huan, is represented here with a rare example of inside painting, signed and dated 'Summer 1825'. The vessel has a disc shape with a long round neck and is painted on the face in *grisaille*, a monochrome painting style rendered in shades of gray to black. The reverse medallion shows the signature, Yifeng, seals of the artist, and the date. In addition, a couplet of fourteen characters refers to the strength of the bamboo grove—according to the inscription it is done after the style of the famous Ming painter, Shen Zhou. Height: 2 1/8 in. (5.3 cm)
Formerly in the collection of Bob C. Stevens.
Exhibited: Mikimoto Hall, Ginza, Tokyo, October 22-31, 1978. Catalogue of the exhibition, *Chinese Snuff Bottles & Dishes: An Exhibition of Chinese Snuff Bottles from the Bob C. Stevens Collection*, p. 99, no. 284.
Illustrated: Stevens, *op. cit.*, no. 830.

■ **181. INSIDE-PAINTED GLASS** by Zhou Leyuan, dated 1889. This early example by the master is signed and dated 'Winter 1889.' It illustrates an elderly gentleman viewing his favorite flower with a young attendant watering plants. The caption on the upper part of the bottle reads: 'I finally have managed to see this illustrious flower in full bloom,' in addition to the name of the artist and the date. The reverse side presents a long passage from the fourth century essay on the Orchid Pavilion. The style and quality of the calligraphy are superior, reflecting the height of Zhou's career as founder of the middle school of inside-painted bottles. Height: 2 7/16 in. (6.2 cm)

■ **182. INSIDE-PAINTED ROCK CRYSTAL** by Zhou Leyuan, dated 1892. The face of this bottle, signed and dated 'Summer 1892,' shows the sweeping yet naturalistic rendering of landscape scenes characteristic of this great artist. A proud rooster prances through a beautiful rocky garden resplendent with large pink peony blossoms which tell us that the scene is one of spring. The cock is also known as a sunbird and carries the emblems of courage and vigilance. Soame Jenyns tells us that 'the cock never forgets the hour.' The reverse shows the familiar scene of a boy playing a flute on the back of a water buffalo, with a windswept tree in the background. The ox or water buffalo is one of the symbolic animals of the Twelve Terrestrial Branches, and in this instance another emblem of spring and agriculture. Height: 2 15/16 in. (5.9 cm)
Illustrated: *Newsletter*, June 1973, p. 12, fig. 24.

■ **183. INSIDE-PAINTED GLASS** by Zhou Leyuan, dated 1892. Here is a montage-like design including a great cauldron; picturesque rockery with *lingzhi* fungus, gnarled tree branches, sprouting prunus blossoms, a pine tree or *penjing* (bonsai); and a wine pot behind. The palette is of muted tones with sepia. The calligraphy in the upper left gives the signature and is dated 'Winter 1892.' The reverse side is of a lone crane under a gnarled pine tree. The sepia tonality of this composition would lead one to believe that winter is fast approaching. The text tells us that the bottle was painted in Beijing in the Studio of the Fragrant Lotus Root. Height: 2 1/2 in. (6.3 cm)

■ **184. INSIDE-PAINTED ROCK CRYSTAL** by Zhou Leyuan, 1885-1890. The painting of this bottle again illustrates the impressionistic style of the artist. The miniature detail of a dragonfly hovering over a water pond with fish darting in every direction contrasts with bold foliage and a lotus flower issuing from the edge of the pond. The scene on the opposite side is in complete contrast to the face, with three windswept trees concealing the pavilion and a lone individual in the landscape. Height: 2 3/8 in. (6.0 cm)

■ **185. INSIDE-PAINTED GLASS** by Ma Shaoxuan, dated 1895. This artist is famous for his montage style of composition. Here two fans show landscapes and water ponds, facsimiles of two stone rubbings minutely detailed, along with a facsimile of calligraphy by Pan Zuyin in the lower right. The reverse side of the bottle has a fifty-character passage from the famous Orchid Pavilion essay by Wang Xizhi. The theme refers to a convocation of the literati. Height: 2 9/16 in. (6.8 cm)
Illustrated: *Newsletter*, June 1973, p. 5, fig. 4.
Illustrated: *Arts of Asia, op. cit.*, p. 33.

■ **186. INSIDE-PAINTED CRYSTAL** by Ma Shaoxuan, dated 1898. Perhaps the most versatile of the inside-painted bottle artists is Ma Shaoxuan. This particular example shows his naturalistic technique with a beautiful rendering of a pavilion, a scholar working at a table, and his attendant. The scholar is poring over his books with the aid of a single candle under a full moon. Flowers are in the foreground as well as a bamboo grove. A large twin pine tree hovers over the pavilion and is drawn in minute detail. Fine calligraphy has always been one of the hallmarks of Ma's bottles, and this is no exception. On the reverse there is a thirty-six character stanza from a famous poem. The clerical script is representative of this artist. Height: 2 1/16 in. (5.2 cm)

■ **187. INSIDE-PAINTED GLASS** by Ma Shaoxuan, dated 1918-1922. This artist was the most prolific portrait painter among all the artists. Here he renders Xu Shichang, the third president of the Republic of China. In fact, the dates on the bottle refer to his ascendency to the presidency and the date he actually resigned, so the bottle is a commemorative one. The reverse side of the vessel includes the following inscription: 'Exhibition of Chinese products at the Kyoto City Product Association.' Height: 2 1/4 in. (5.8 cm)
Illustrated: *JICSBS*, December 1978, p. 11, fig. 34.

■ **188. INSIDE-PAINTED GLASS** by Ma Shaoxuan, dated 'Spring 1899.' The two sisters on an elegant settee is a theme that the artist repeated many, many times. The quality of the painting, its costumes and the colors, warrant its inclusion in this catalogue. On the reverse side is a poem that answers some of the questions raised by this picturesque scene. The text reads:

> The sisters Qiao read a book together.
> Both married to handsome men and heroes of the time.
> On such a fine night, why are they not sleeping?
> Because they, too, love to read books on warfare strategies.

Height: 2 7/16 in. (6.2 cm)
Illustrated: *JICSBS*, September 1978, p. 16, face and reverse.

■ **189. INSIDE-PAINTED GLASS** by Meng Zishou, dated 'Summer 1909.' Thanks to the scholarship of Emily Byrne Curtis, we can definitely identify the portrait on this bottle as that of the Manzu General Feng Shan. The distinctive quality of this portrait ranks the artist's work with the finest produced by Ma Shaoxuan. The inscription on the reverse side is in five different styles of calligraphy. The translation reads as follows:

> (Top right) Cool and at ease, as was He Zhizhang
> Prosperous and favored, as was Guo Fenyang
> With numerous descendants inheriting one's literary fame
> And the old do not grow old but live in health and longevity.
>
> (Bottom right) Don't say that the world inside the bottle is small
> It allows one to give up the world of care
> As if escaping to a wonder land
>
> (Top left) Written on a summer day of 1909 at the Xigu Shanfang in the capital.
> Zishou, Meng Zhaoxun.
>
> (Bottom left) Archaic script with ordinary script above it,
> a partial translation of which reads:
> By order of heaven three times,
> Long life and glory to the Emperor.

Height: 2 3/16 in. (5.6 cm)
Illustrated and translated: Emily Byrne Curtis, *Reflected Glory in a Bottle, Chinese Snuff Bottle Portraits*, Soho Bodhi, New York, 1980. Text on p. 19 and illustrated on pps. 78, 79.

■ **190. INSIDE-PAINTED GLASS** by Zi Yizi. This artist rendered many versions of the famous General Huang Zhong. He is here shown with a long white beard and a face framed by dragon banners in tones of gold and orange. The important Beijing actor portraying the general was Tan Xinpei, the most celebrated actor of the day, especially in the roles of elderly dignified gentlemen and generals. The reverse side is an unexpected surprise in that most bottles by this artist include a long poem about the general; however, this one has a lovely garden scene with a bronze vessel, gnarled wood, prunus blossoms, and peonies. Height: 2 9/16 in. (6.8 cm)
Illustrated: *JICSBS*, June 1977, p. 19

180   181   182   183

184   185   186

187   188   189   190

Description

■ **191. INSIDE-PAINTED GLASS** by Ye Zhongsan the Elder, dated to the 'second autumn month of 1892.' One of the most prolific of the inside-painted artists, the elder Ye Zhongsan did his first mature painting in the early 1890s. Here the master rendered a delicate scene of lotus stalks and flowers with a large black and white bird drawn in naturalistic style. The reverse side is more impressionistic, with two large windblown willow trees and a boy, playing a flute, seated on a water buffalo somewhat submerged in the water and underneath massive trees. In the foreground are rocks and a rustic wooden bridge. Height: 2 1/2 in. (6.3 cm)

■ **192. INSIDE-PAINTED CHALCEDONY** by Ye Zhongsan the Younger, dated 'Autumn 1917.' The conception, material, and design are the same as a bottle Hugh Moss published in his *Snuff Bottles of China*, no. 381. The cloudy texture of the semi-transparent chalcedony acts as foil for fantailed goldfish, in black and red, swimming about the edges of a simulated goldfish bowl. The artist's conception reminds one of the beautiful goldfish ponds seen in Chinese gardens in the East and the West. Height: 2 1/2 in. (6.3 cm)

■ **193. INSIDE-PAINTED ROCK CRYSTAL** by Ye Zhongsan the Elder, dated 'Summer 1895.' The year marks the beginning of the mature period of the artist, and this bottle is a good demonstration of that style. The vessel is individualized by a continuous scene wrapping around the entire flattened form. A panoramic landscape of mountains, lakes, streams, and trees affords glimpses of a boatman and figures crossing a bridge. The backdrop on the reverse side is heightened by horizontal bands of scuttling clouds. Height: 2 9/16 in. (6.5 cm)

■ **194. INSIDE-PAINTED GLASS** by Ye Zhongsan. This bottle is not signed, but the style and quality are so distinctive that Hugh Moss and other scholars all concur that it is by the elder Ye. The theme is that of the hundred children. In this instance, the rocky garden is filled with children in animated poses which symbolize the desire for fertility and descendants. The reverse side shows the famous wutong tree (*elocococca*), a tree the Chinese love and the only tree on which the famous phoenix will alight. If such a bottle were given as a gift to another person, it would symbolize the desire for progeny or its fulfillment. Height: 2 7/16 in. (6.2 cm)
Illustrated: Perry, *op. cit.*, p. 139. no. 143.
Illustrated: *Newsletter*, June 1973, p. 9, fig. 15.

■ **195. INSIDE-PAINTED ROCK CRYSTAL** by Ye Zhongsan the Elder, dated 1909. The scene is entitled 'Heavenly Maidens.' It refers to Shennu (a goddess) who befriended a man named Mi, as he was lost in the mountains and needed money to continue his journey. The illustrations on each side show the chance encounter between Shennu, with her heavenly maidens, and Mi. (See V. Mead's article in *JICSBS*, September 1980, p. 16.) Added distinction is given to this bottle by relief carving of a tree trunk, helping to define the inside-painted scene. Height: 3 1/16 in. (7.7 cm)
Formerly in the collection of Martin Schoen.
Exhibited: China Institute. Catalogue, no. 37.
Illustrated: *JICSBS*, September 1980, p. 16.

■ **196. INSIDE-PAINTED GLASS** by Chen Zhongsan, dated 'Summer 1912.' No artist has produced finer examples of woodland scenes with insects amid vegetation. Magnification is required to fully appreciate the details this artist renders with utmost care, even to the point of creating spider webs on one side. Below the branches are two butterflies, a cicada, crickets with a praying mantis, a grasshopper on a gnarled rock, and a Chinese cabbage, *baicai*, with a ladybug on it. Height: 2 9/16 in. (6.5 cm)

■ **197. INSIDE-PAINTED GLASS** by Ding Erzhong, 1896-1900—Ding, one of the consummate artists of the middle school, produced a small number of bottles, but each is distinguished by his imagination and skill. This example shows a phoenix in an impressionistic sunset landscape. The brush strokes are rendered in such manner as to add a degree of tension and drama to the scene. The reverse side, including the signature but no date, is of a simple rocky garden landscape with the early spring symbols of prunus and peony blossoms. Height: 2 1/4 in. (5.7 cm)
Formerly in the collection of Ralph M. Hults.

■ **198. INSIDE-PAINTED GLASS** by Gui Xianggu, dated 'Summer 1896.' This oblong bottle includes four ovoid-shaped panels. Two faces are painted in sepia tones with a crane under a pine tree on one face and fantailed red and black goldfishes in a murky pond on the opposite side. The side panels give this bottle its special character; one relates that the vessel was given to Zhiqing by the painter. The other states that the bottle was painted at Beijing in the summer of 1896. Height: 2 3/8 in. (6.0 cm)

■ **199. INSIDE-PAINTED GLASS** by Meng Zishou, dated 'Summer 1908.' The same artist who created the portrait bottle, no. 189, is also the originator of this design. The painter's work is difficult to find but is distinctive as is seen in this example. The aquatic scene is replete with large and small carp and goldfish swimming amid flowering lotus plants of imposing size, running in a continuous scene around the bottle. Height: 2 3/8 in. (6.0 cm)
Formerly in the collection of Ralph M. Hults.

■ **200. INSIDE-PAINTED ROCK CRYSTAL** by Wang Xisan, dated 'Winter 1973.' The bottle was undoubtedly fabricated at an earlier date and carved in low relief detailing mountains and trees which serve as a foil for the inside painting by the most famous modern artist. Wang has used the impurities within the crystal to reveal white and ice-like textures. Enveloping the entire bottle, this late winter and early spring picture with magnificent prunus boughs and budding blossoms is enhanced by a subtle use of color. The poem is about the beautiful flowering prunus amid the snow. The actual title given on one face is 'Winter Prunus.' The inscription follows: *Yihuzhai zhi*, meaning 'made by The One Pot Studio.' Height: 2 5/16 in. (5.9 cm)

191
192
193
194
195
196
197
198
199
200

Description

- **2.** *See description on page 28*
- **17.** *See description on page 30*
- **9.** *See description on page 28*
- **45.** *See description on page 38*
- **38.** *See description on page 36*
- **76.** *See description on page 46*
- **103.** *See description on page 52*
- **132.** *See description on page 58*
- **152.** *See description on page 62*

2

17

9

45

38

76

103

132

152

Selected Bibliography

Ayers, John. 'Chinese Glass.' In *Arts of the Ch'ing Dynasty*, pp. 17-27. London: Oriental Ceramic Society, 1965.

Beurdeley, Cécile and Michel. *Giuseppe Castiglione: A Jesuit Painter at the Court of the Chinese Emperors*. Translated by Michael Bullock. Rutland, Vermont, and Tokyo: Tuttle, 1977.

Beurdeley, Jean-Michel. *The Chinese Collector through the Centuries*. Rutland, Vermont, and Tokyo: Tuttle, 1966.

Börner, Rudolf. *Minerals, Rocks and Gemstones*. Edinburgh: Oliver & Boyd, 1966.

Cammann, Schuyler. *Land of the Camel*. New York: 1951.

_____. *China's Dragon Robes*. New York: Ronald Press, 1952.

_____. 'The Story of Hornbill Ivory.' *University Museum Bulletin* (University of Pennsylvania), December 1950, pp. 19-47.

_____. 'Chinese Mandarin Squares.' *University Museum Bulletin* (University of Pennsylvania), June 1953.

_____. 'Chinese "Eglomisé" Snuff-Bottles.' *Oriental Art*, Autumn 1957, pp. 85-89.

_____. 'Chinese Inside-Painted Snuff Bottles and Their Makers.' *Harvard Journal of Asiatic Studies* 10 (1957): 295-326.

_____. 'Substance and Symbol in Chinese Snuff Bottles—Part I.' *Journal of the International Chinese Snuff Bottle Society*, March 1976, pp. 3-11.

_____. 'Substance and Symbol in Chinese Snuff Bottles—Part II.' *Journal of the International Chinese Snuff Bottle Society*, June 1976, pp. 14-22.

_____. 'Chinese Snuff Bottles as Viewed by Some Old Chinese Scholars—Part I.' *Journal of the International Chinese Snuff Bottle Society*, June 1980, pp. 4-7.

_____. 'Chinese Snuff Bottles as Viewed by Some Old Chinese Scholars—Part II.' *Journal of the International Chinese Snuff Bottle Society*, December 1980, pp. 10-12 and 35.

Chang, Lin-sheng. 'Painted Enamel Snuff Bottles of the Ch'ing Dynasty.' *Journal of the International Chinese Snuff Bottle Society*, March 1977, pp. 4-12 and 37-39.

China Institute in America. *Exhibition of Chinese Snuff Bottles of the Seventeenth and Eighteenth Centuries from the Collection of Mr. and Mrs. Martin Schoen*. New York, 1952. Catalogue of an exhibition held December 1, 1952-January 31, 1953.

Chow, Fong. 'Symbolism in Chinese Porcelain: The Rockefeller Bequest.' *Metropolitan Museum of Art Bulletin*, Summer 1962, pp. 12-24.

Christie, Anthony. *Chinese Mythology*. London: Hamlyn, 1968.

Coullery, Marie-Thérèse. 'Flacons à tabac chinois.' *Collections Baur*, Autumn-Winter 1973, pp. 2-13. Translated in the *Newsletter of the Chinese Snuff Bottle Society of America*, March 1974, pp. 5-14.

_____. 'Flacons à tabac en verre doublé à technique de camée.' *Collections Baur*, Autumn-Winter 1972, pp. 10-15. Translated in the *Newsletter of the Chinese Snuff Bottle Society of America*, September 1973, pp. 8-9.

Curtis, Emily Byrne. *Reflected Glory in a Bottle: Chinese Snuff Bottle Portraits*. New York: Soho Bodhi, 1980.

_____. 'The Impact of the West—Part One, China in the Nineteenth Century.' *Journal of the International Chinese Snuff Bottle Society*, June 1981, pp. 5-12.

du Boulay, Anthony. 'The Development of Porcelain in Relation to Snuff Bottles.' *Journal of the International Chinese Snuff Bottle Society*, March 1980, pp. 5-9.

Feddersen, Martin. *Chinese Decorative Art: A Handbook for Collectors and Connoisseurs*. New York: Yoseloff, 1961.

Ford, John. 'Edward O'Dell's Collection.' *Arts of Asia*, November-December 1976, pp. 31-37.

_____. 'Edward Choate O'Dell—A Memorial Tribute.' *Journal of the International Chinese Snuff Bottle Society*, Summer 1982, pp. 5-11.

Garner, Harry. *Chinese and Japanese Cloisonné Enamels*. 1962.

Goodrich, L. Carrington. *A Short History of the Chinese People*. New York: Harper, 1943.

Hackin, J., and others. *Asiatic Mythology*. New York: Crescent Books, 1963.

Hamilton, W. R.; Wooley, A. R.; and Bishop, A. C. *Hamlyn Guide to Minerals, Rocks and Fossils*. London: Hamlyn, 1974.

Hansford, S. Howard. *Chinese Jade Carvings*. London: Lund Humphries, 1950. Greenwich, Conn.: New York Graphic Society, 1968.

_____. 'Jade and Jade Carvings in the Ch'ing Dynasty.' In *Arts of the Ch'ing Dynasty*, pp. 29-39. London: Oriental Ceramic Society, 1965.

Hardy, Sheila Yorke. 'Ku Yüeh Hsüan—A New Hypothesis.' *Oriental Art*, Winter 1949-50, pp. 116-25.

Hartman, Joan M. *Chinese Jade in Five Centuries*. Rutland, Vermont, and Tokyo: Tuttle, 1969.

Hitt, Henry C. *Old Chinese Snuff Bottles*. Bremerton, Washington: privately printed, 1945. Rutland, Vermont, and Tokyo: Tuttle, 1978.

Huish, Marcus B. *Chinese Snuff Bottles of Stone, Porcelain and Glass*. London: Chiswick Press, 1895.

_____. 'A Little Appreciated Side of Art—Chinese Snuff Bottles.' *Studio*, June 1896, pp. 11-16.

Hurlbut, Cornelius S. 'Some Minerals Fashioned into Snuff Bottles.' *Newsletter of the Chinese Snuff Bottle Society of America*, December 1972, p. 13-20.

Jenyns, Soame. *Chinese Art.* Vol. 4, The Minor Arts II. New York: Universe Books, 1965.

———. *Background to Chinese Painting.* London: Sedgwick & Jackson, 1935. New York: Schocken, 1966.

———. *Later Chinese Porcelain: The Ch'ing Dynasty.* Faber & Faber, 1971.

Journal of the International Chinese Snuff Bottle Society (referred to as: *JICSBS*).

Jutheau, Viviane. 'Lacquer Snuff Bottles.' *Journal of the International Chinese Snuff Bottle Society,* June 1981, pp. 20-23 and 31.

Lee, James Zee-min. *Chinese Potpourri.* Hong Kong: Oriental Publishers, 1950.

Li, Raymond. *Snuff Bottle Terminology: Chinese and English Equivalents, Part I—Glass, Agate, Quartz.* Hong Kong: Nine Dragons, 1981.

Loehr, Max. 'Subject-Matter in the Decor of Snuff Bottles.' *Newsletter of the Chinese Snuff Bottle Society of America,* June 1973, pp. 4-14.

Mayer, Marian. *Glass Snuff Bottles of China from the Mayer Collection.* Falmouth, Mass.: CommuniGraphics, 1981. Catalogue of an exhibition held at Steuben Glass, September 9-October 3, 1980.

Mead, Virginia. 'The Confucian Women.' *Journal of the International Chinese Snuff Bottle Society,* September 1978, pp. 12-18.

———. 'A Guide to Chinese Snuff Bottles from the *Liao Chai Chi I:* English Story Adaptations Based on Translations by Jean Yu.' *Journal of the International Chinese Snuff Bottle Society;* September 1980, pp. 1-37.

Medley, Margaret. *Handbook of Chinese Art for Collectors and Students.* London: Bell, 1964. New York: Horizon Press, 1972.

Moss, Hugh M. *Chinese Snuff Bottles of the Silica or Quartz Group.* London: Bibelot, 1971.

———. *Snuff Bottles of China.* London: Bibelot, 1971.

———. *By Imperial Command: An Introduction to Ch'ing Imperial Painted Enamels.* Hong Kong: Hibiya Co. Ltd, 1976.

———. ed. *Chinese Snuff-Bottles.* No. 1, 1963; No. 2, 1964; No. 3, 1965; No. 4, 1966; No. 5, 1969; No. 6, 1974.

———. *Chinese Snuff Bottles in the Fitzwilliam Museum.* London: Moss (Publications) Ltd., 1974.

———. 'An Imperial Habit—Part I.' *Journal of the International Chinese Snuff Bottle Society,* December 1975, pp. 3-15.

———. 'An Imperial Habit—Part II.' *Journal of the International Chinese Snuff Bottle Society,* March 1976, pp. 12-21

———. 'A Confusion of Modern Bottles.' *Journal of the International Chinese Snuff Bottle Society,* September 1977, pp. 9-18.

———. 'A Guide to Marks on Chinese Ceramics of the Ming and Ch'ing Dynasties—Part I.' *Journal of the International Chinese Snuff Bottle Society,* June 1978, pp. 26-37.

———. 'Enameled Glass Wares of the Ku Yüeh Hsüan Group.' *Journal of the International Chinese Snuff Bottle Society,* June 1978, pp. 5-25.

———. 'European Influence on the Ch'ing Imperial Workshop.' *Connoisseur,* January 1975, pp. 41-45. Reprinted in *Journal of the International Chinese Snuff Bottle Society,* March 1979, pp. 25-29.

———. 'The Apricot Grove Studio, The Ye Family of Snuff Bottle Artists.' *Journal of the International Chinese Snuff Bottle Society,* Spring 1982, pp. 1-8

Moss, Hugh M. and Moss, Paul. 'A Guide to Marks on Chinese Ceramics of the Ming and Ch'ing Dynasties—Part II.' *Journal of the International Chinese Snuff Bottle Society,* September 1978, pp. 19-29.

Munsterberg, Hugo. *Dragons in Chinese Art.* New York: China Institute in America, 1972. Catalogue of an exhibition held March 23-May 28, 1972.

National Palace Museum. *Masterpieces of Chinese Miniature Crafts in the National Palace Museum.* Taipei, 1971.

National Palace Museum. *Masterpieces of Chinese Snuff-Bottles in the National Palace Museum.* Taipei, 1974.

Newsletter of the Chinese Snuff Bottle Society of America (referred to as: *Newsletter*).

Nott, Stanley Charles. *Chinese Culture in the Arts: Being an Illustrated Descriptive Record of the Meaning of the Emblematic and Symbolic Designs Personified in the Arts of China throughout the Ages.* New York: Chinese Culture Study Group of America, 1946.

Perry, Lilla S. *Chinese Snuff Bottles: The Adventures and Studies of a Collector.* Rutland, Vermont, and Tokyo: Tuttle, 1960.

Reilly, Theresa M. 'Chinese Jewelry and its Relation to Snuff Bottles.' *Journal of the International Chinese Snuff Bottle Society,* March 1981, pp. 5-11 and 20.

Schneeberger, P. F. 'Note sur un flacon à tabac émaillé.' *Collections Baur,* Autumn-Winter 1973, pp. 14-16. Translated in the *Newsletter of the Chinese Snuff Bottle Society of America,* March 1974, pp. 15-16.

Stevens, Bob C. *The Collector's Book of Snuff Bottles.* New York and Tokyo: Weatherhill, 1976.

———. *Chinese Snuff Bottles & Dishes: An Exhibition of Chinese Snuff Bottles from the Bob C. Stevens Collection.* Tokyo: Mikimoto Co., 1978. Catalogue of an exhibition held October 22-October 31, 1978.

———. 'Chinese Snuff Bottles "Made in Japan."' *Arts of Asia,* July-August 1973, pp. 41-45.

———. 'Yi-hsing Snuff Bottles.' *Arts of Asia,* September-October 1973, pp. 43-46.

———. 'Questions and Answers.' *Journal of the International Chinese Snuff Bottle Society,* June 1975, p. 22.

Sowerby, Arthur. *Nature in Chinese Art.* New York: John Day, 1940.

Sullivan, Michael. *The Art of China.* London: Faber & Faber, 1967.

Tsang, Gerard C. C. *Chinese Snuff Bottles.* Hong Kong: Hong Kong Museum of Art, 1977. Catalogue of an exhibition held October 15-November 26, 1977.

———. 'Yangchou Seal Bottles.' *Journal of the International Chinese Snuff Bottle Society,* June 1979, pp. 5-10.

Tsang, Gerard C. C. and Moss, Hugh. *Snuff Bottles of the Ch'ing Dynasty.* Hong Kong: Hong Kong Museum of Art, 1978. Catalogue of an exhibition held October 20-December 3, 1978.

Warner, Marina. *The Dragon Empress.* Great Britain: Weidenfeld & Nicholson Ltd., 1972.

Watt, James C. Y. *Chinese Jades from Han to Ch'ing.* New York: The Asia Society Inc., 1980.

Webster, Robert. *The Gemologists' Compendium.* London: NAG Press, 5th rev. ed., 1970. Orig. pub. 1938.

Werner, E. T. C. *Dictionary of Chinese Mythology.* Shanghai: Kelly & Walsh, 1932. New York: Julian Press, 1961.

Williams, C. A. S. *Encyclopedia of Chinese Symbolism and Art Motives.* New York: Julian Press, 1960.

Glossary

Pinyin/(Wade-Giles)   Chinese Characters   English

Aomen   (Ao-mên)   澳門   Macao

Aomen jilue   (Ao-mên chi-lüeh)   澳門紀略   *A History of Macao*

Baishi   (Pai-shih)   白石   'White Stone,' artist's seal

baicai   (pai-ts'ai)   白菜   Chinese cabbage

baitong   (pai-tung)   白銅   Chinese white brass

baoxianghua   (pao hsiang hua)   寶相花   precious image flower

baxian   (pa-hsien)   八仙   Eight Immortals

Beijing   (Pei-ching)   北京   Peking

Bi-yan cong-ke   (Pi-yen ts'ung-k'o)   鼻煙叢刻   publication on snuff

Boshan   (Po-shan)   博山   city

Chen Zhongsan   (Ch'en Chung-san)   陳仲三   inside-painted artist

Cheng Rongzhang   (Ch'eng Jung-chang)   程榮章   porcelain carver

Cheng Ziqing   (Ch'eng Tzu-tsing)   程子青   maker's name

chilong   (ch'ih-lung)   螭龍   archaic dragon

Danshan   (Tan-shan)   丹山   'Cinnabar Mountain,' maker's name

Daoguang   (Tao-kuang)   道光   emperor's reign 1821-1850

Daoist   (Taoist)   道家   religion or philosophy

Daoxue xunmei   (Tao-hsüeh hsun-mei)   踏雪尋梅   Searching for plum blossoms in the snow

ding   (ting)   鼎   bronze tripod vessel

Ding Erzhong   (Ting Erh-chung)   丁二仲   inside-painted artist

dou-yan   (tou-yen)   豆烟   snuff of the second grade

dui   (tui)   敦   type of vessel

Fang Yizhi   (Fang I-chih)   方以智   author

fei-yan   (fei-yen)   飛烟   snuff of the first grade

feicui   (fei-ts'ui)   翡翠   gem quality jade

fo   (foo or fu)   佛   Buddha or Buddhist

foshou   (fo shou)   佛手   Buddha's hand, citron

Fujian   (Fukien)   福建   province

Gan Huan   (Kan Huan)   甘桓   inside-painted artist

Gao Shiji   (Kao Shih-ch'i)   高士奇   Kangxi's personal secretary

Gu-xue Hui-kan   (Ku-hsüeh Hui-k'an)   古學彙刊   Publications on classics

Guangdong (Kuangtung) 廣東 province

Guangdong Tongzhi *(Kuang-tung T'ung-chih)* 廣東通志 *Guangdong Provincial Gazette*

Guangzhou (Kuang-chou) 廣州 Canton

Gui Xianggu (Kuei Hsiang-ku) 桂香谷 inside-painted artist

Guo Fenyang (Kuo Fen-yang) 郭汾陽 name of a person

Gusongxuan (Ku-sung Hsüan) 古松軒 Ancient Pine Studio

Guyuexuan Ku-yüeh Hsüan 古月軒 Ancient Moon Pavilion

Hao Yulin (Hao Yu-lin) 郝玉麟 author

He Zhizhang (Ho Chih-chang) 賀知章 name of a person

Heshen (Ho-shên) 和珅 Qianlong's minister

He Xiangu (Ho Hsien-ku) 何仙姑 lady Daoist Immortal

Huang Zhong (Huang Chung) 黃忠 general and popular Beijing opera role

Jiade (Chia-tê) 家德 master carver's name

Jiangsu (Kiangsu) 江蘇 province

Jiangxi (Kiangsi) 江西 province

Jiaqing (Chia-ch'ing) 嘉慶 emperor's reign 1796-1820

Jiaqing nianzhi (Chia-ch'ing nien chih) 嘉慶年製 made in the Jiaqing period

Jingdezhen (Ching-tê Chên) 景德鎮 city, porcelain center

jingzhi (ching-chih) 敬製 respectfully made

jinshi (chin-shih) 進士 successful candidate in the highest imperial examinations

Jiqing (Chi-ch'ing) 吉慶 viceroy of Guangzhou

jiyou (chi-yu) 己酉 cyclical date (1849)

Juji (Chü-chi) 聚記 studio mark

kang (k'ang) 炕 brick bed warmed by fire

Kangxi (K'ang-hsi) 康熙 emperor's reign 1662-1722

Lanpo of Wumen (Lan-po of Wu-men) 吳門蘭坡 carver's name

lingzhi (ling-chih) 靈芝 fungus of immortality

Liu Hai (Liu Hai) 劉海 young Immortal

liuli (liu-li) 琉璃 translucent or opaque glass

Li Xu (Li Hsü) 李煦 textile commissioner at Suzhou

Luohan (Lohan) 羅漢 Arhat or Buddhist saint

Ma Shaoxuan (Ma Shao-hsüan) 馬少宣 inside-painted artist

Manzu　(Manchu)　满族　race

Mengjian　(Mêng-chien)　孟堅　artist's name

Meng Zhaoxun　(Mêng Chao-hsun)　孟昭勲　inside-painted artist [pen name: Zishou]

Meng Zishou　(Mêng Tzǔ-shou)　孟子受　Meng Zhaoxum's pen name

Ming　(Ming)　明　dynasty (1368-1644)

Mu Wang　(Mu Wang)　穆王　Zhou dynasty ruler

Mulan　(Mulan)　木蘭　heroine's name

Nanjing　(Nan-ching)　南京　Nanking, city

Pan Zuyin　(P'an Tsu-yin)　潘祖蔭　calligrapher's name

Pengshan Miji　*(Peng-shan Mi-chi)*　蓬山密記　*Private Notes from Pengshan*

penjing　(pan-ching)　盆景　bonsai

Qi-ying　(Ch'i-ying)　耆英　imperial commissioner at Guangzhou

Qianlong　(Ch'ien-lung)　乾隆　emperor's reign 1736-1795

Qianlong nianzhi　(Ch'ien-lung nien chih)　乾隆年製　made in the Qianlong period

Qianlong yuti　(Ch'ien-lung yu ti)　乾隆御題　composed by Qianlong

qilin　(ch'i-lin)　麒麟　Chinese unicorn

qin　(chin)　琴　Chinese zither

Qing　(Ch'ing)　清　dynasty (1644-1912)

renshen　(jên-shên)　壬申　cyclical date (1872)

Runsheng　(Jun-shêng)　潤生　artist's signature

ruyi　(ju-i)　如意　scepter

San-ba Ji　*(San-pa Chi)*　三巴集　*Collection of Poems from São Paulo*

Shandong　(Shantung)　山東　province

Shanghai　(Shanghai)　上海　city

Shennu　(Shen Nü)　神女　Goddess

Shen Zhou　(Shen Chou)　沈周　Ming dynasty painter (pen name: Shitian)

Shenyang　(Shên-yang)　瀋陽　Mukden

Shitian　(Shih-t'ien)　石田　Shen Zhou's pen name

Shixiang　(Shih-hsiang)　石香　artist's name

shou　(shou)　壽　longevity

Shoulao　(Shou-lao)　壽老　God of Longevity

Shunzhi　(Shun-chih)　順治　emperor's reign 1644-1661

Sui-luan Ji-en (Sui-luan Chi-en) 隨輦紀恩 Publication in the *Xiao-fang-hu-zhai Yu-ti Cong-chao*

Suzhou (Suchou) 蘇州 Soochow, city

tan-ba-gu yiancao (tan-pa-ku yien-ts'ao) 淡把姑烟草 tobacco plant

Tan Xinpei (T'an Hsin-p'ei) 譚鑫培 Beijing opera actor

taoliao (t'ao-liao) 套料 overlaid colors

taotie (t'ao-t'ieh) 饕餮 animal mask

Tongzhi (T'ung-chih) 同治 emperor's reign 1862-1874

Wanli (Wan-li) 萬歷 emperor's reign 1573-1619

Wan-shou Sheng-dian Chu-ji (Wan-shou Sheng-tien Ch'u-chi) 萬壽盛典初集 *Initial Chronicle of the Royal Grand Ceremony*

Wang Bingrong (Wang Ping-jung) 王炳榮 artist's name

Wang Hao (Wang Hao) 汪灝 author

Wang Hongxu (Wang Hung-hsü) 王鴻緒 Chinese courtier

Wang Shizhen (Wang Shih-chên) 王士禛 author

Wang Shixiong (Wang Shih-hsiung) 王世雄 enamel artist

Wang Xiqi (Wang Shih-chi) 王錫祺 author

Wang Xisan (Wang Hsi-san) 王習三 inside-painted artist

Wang Xizhi (Wang Hsi-chih) 王羲之 'Orchid pavilion' author

Weijian (Wei-chien) 味劍 name of person for whom snuff bottle was carved by Lanpo of Wumen

Wenshan ke (Wen-shan k'ê) 文山刻 carved by Wenshan

Wu Li (Wu Li) 吳歷 master painter of early Qing dynasty and snuff user

Wu-li Xiao-shi (Wu-li Hsiao-shih) 物理小識 Encyclopedic publication

wufu linmen (wu fu lin men) 五福臨門 May the five blessings visit you.

wutong (wu-tung) 梧桐 Chinese tree

Xi-zhao Ding-an (Hsi-ch'ao Ting-an) 熙朝定案 Publication from the Imperial Court

Xiang-zu Bi-ji (Hsiang-tsu Pi-chi) 香祖筆記 *Notes from Xiang-zu*

Xiao-fang-hu-zhai Yu-ti Cong-chao (Hsiao-fang-hu-chai Yu-ti T'sung-ch'ao) 小方壺齋輿地叢鈔 *Collection from the Little-Square-Pot-Studio Territory*

Xigu Shanfang (Hsi-ku Shan-fang) 習古山房 studio name

Xing-you heng-tang (Hsing-yu heng-t'ang) 行有恆堂 Hall of Constancy

Xiwangmu (Hsi Wang Mu) 西王母 Queen Mother of the West

Xu Shichang (Hsu Shih-ch'ang) 徐世昌 Third president of the Republic of China

yang (yang) 陽 male, active, positive principle

Yangzhou hua-fang lu (Yang-chou hua-fan lu) 揚州畫舫錄 publication

Ye (Yeh) 葉 family name of inside-painted artists

Ye Zhongsan (Yeh Chung-san) 葉仲三 inside-painted artist

Yifeng (I-fêng) 一峰 artist's signature (pen name)

Yijinzhai (I-chin Chai) 詒晉齋 studio name

Yihuzhai zhi (I-hu Chai chih) 一壺齋製 made by The One Pot Studio

Yijing (I-ching) 易經 The Book of Changes

yin (yin) 陰 female, passive, negative principle

Yin Guangren (Yin Kuang-jên) 印光任 author

Yixing (I-hsing) 宜興 city, type of stoneware, ceramic center

Yong-lu xian-jie (Yung-lu hsien-chieh) 勇盧閒詰 Leisure Enquiries into Snuff

Yongxing (Yung-hsing) 永瑆 first Prince Cheng 1752-1823

Yongzheng (Yung-chêng) 雍正 emperor's reign 1723-1735

Yongzheng nianzhi (Yung-chêng nien chih) 雍正年製 made in the Yongzheng period

Zaiquan (Tsai-chüan) 載銓 fifth Prince Ting

Zhang Jiebin (Chang Chieh-pin) 張介賓 physician

Zhang Rulin (Chang Ju-lin) 張汝霖 author

Zhao Zhiqian (Chao Chih-ch'ien) 趙之謙 author of the first book on snuff and snuff bottles

Zhejiang (Chekiang) 浙江 province

zhi lan (chih lan) 芝蘭 fungi and orchids

Zhiqing (Chih-ch'ing) 贒卿 name of person receiving snuff bottle from Gui Xianggu

Zhou (Chou) 周 dynasty (1122-256 B.C.)

Zhou Leyuan (Chou Lo-yüan) 周樂元 inside-painted artist

Zhu Xiqing (Chu Hsi-ch'ing) 朱夕清 maker's name

zhuangxin qianli (chuang-hsin ch'ien li) 壯心千里 Traveling 1,000 miles with a stout heart

Zi Yizi (Tzǔ I-tzǔ) 自怡子 inside-painted artist

Zishou (Tzǔ-shou) 子受 Meng Zhaoxun's pen name

zitan (tzǔ-tan) 紫檀 sandalwood

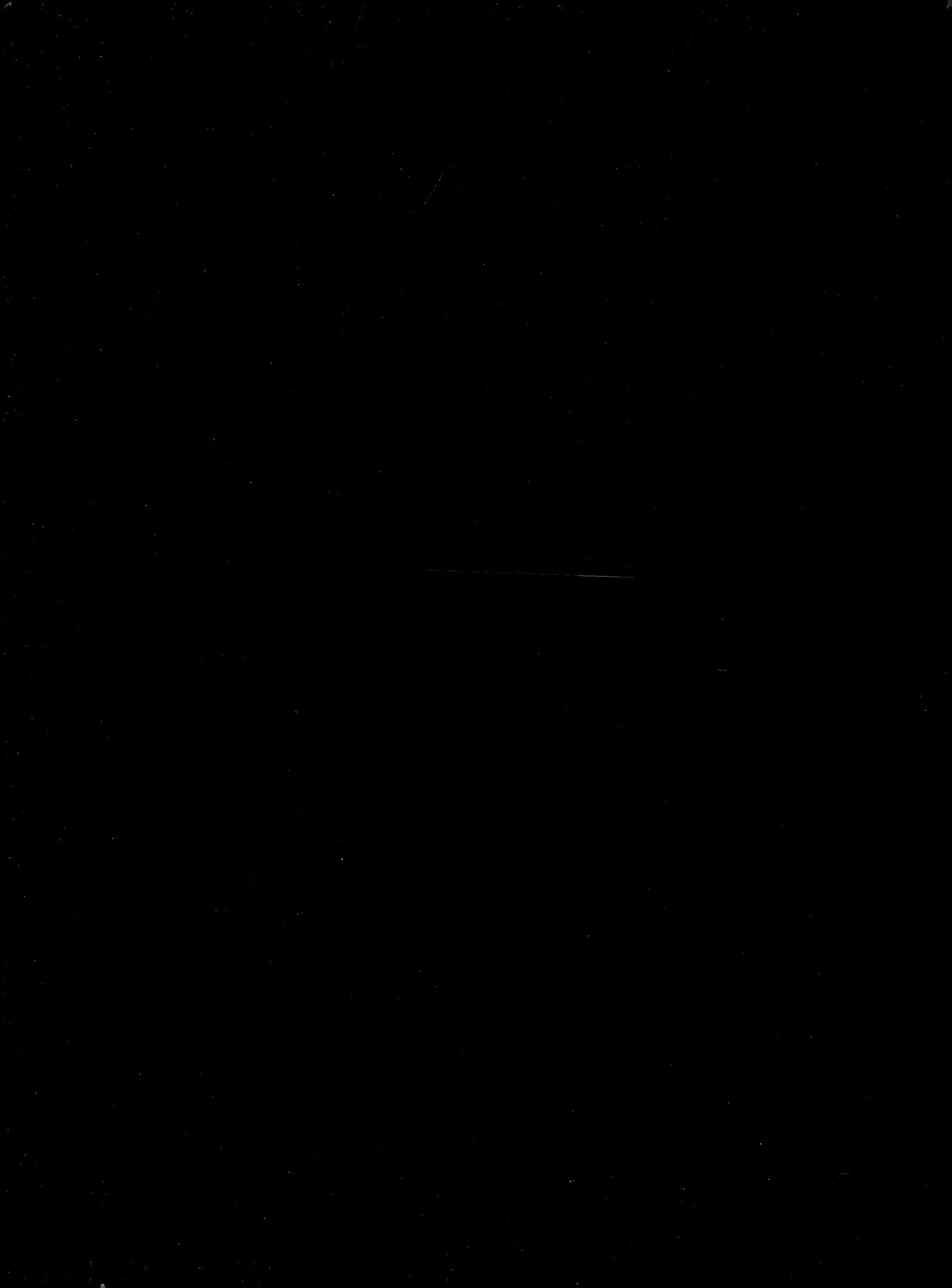